MENTAL SPEED BUMPS

The smarter way to tame traffic

All the best
David

envirobook

Copyright © 2005 David Engwicht
First edition.

National Library of Australia
Cataloguing-in-Publication Entry

Engwicht, David, 1950- .
Mental speed bumps : the smarter way to tame traffic.

ISBN 0 85881 209 6.

1. Engwicht, David, 1950- . 2. Traffic engineering.
3. Traffic safety. 4. City Planning. I. Title.

388.41312

Illustrations & Layout: David Engwicht.
Cover: David Engwicht & Diane McIntosh.
Set in Adobe Caslon Pro 10/14.

Published by *Envirobook*
38 Rose Street, Annandale, NSW 2038. Australia.
Telephone 02 9518 6154
Printed in China by Bookbuilders.

Copies available online at: **www.mentalspeedbumps.com**

To the 'Sarah' who lives in the imagination of us all.

Content

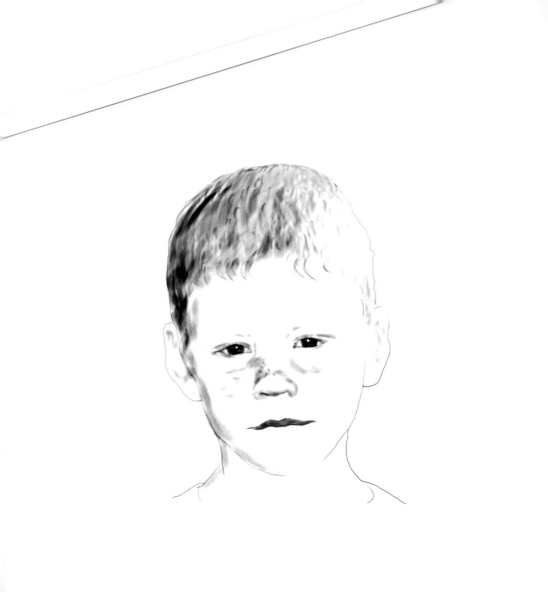

PART 1

The Simultaneous Discovery

Can a street party really slow traffic, even weeks after it has finished?

The Accidental Discovery in Henry Street

I made an accidental discovery in 1996 that turned everything I believed about streets and calming traffic upside down. Brisbane City Council agreed to trial an idea I called the Traffic Reduction Treaty. Neighbourhoods would exchange a treaty with each other. It read: 'We will drive slower and act like a guest in your neighbourhood if you do the same for us'. I suggested to the city that no neighbourhood should get traffic calming unless they first signed this treaty.

At this stage I still believed passionately in traffic calming, having written a traffic calming booklet that is credited with helping to spark a traffic calming revolution in parts of Australia and North America. However, by this stage I was arguing that we needed a new generation of traffic calming. Instead of using negative devices (like speed bumps) to force motorists into slowing down, I advocated using positive devices (like play areas for kids). I still believed that these positive-oriented devices needed to change the physical geometry of the street in order to force motorists into slowing down.

Henry Street was selected for the trial of the Traffic Reduction Treaty. In phase one we would educate the residents about clever ways to fulfil their commitments to the Traffic Reduction Treaty. For example, we showed them ways that they could manage their car use much more efficiently so they were putting less traffic in other neighbourhoods. In phase two we would work with the residents to redesign their street using second generation traffic calming techniques. These works would be a reward for them taking responsibility for their own car use.

At the end of phase one we had a giant street party to celebrate the fact that during a test week, the Henry Street residents had reduced their car use by a massive 34%. A short time after the street party, I met with the residents to review the project and plan for the next stage – traffic calming their street. Some of the residents were very excited about the outcomes of phase one.

'The traffic is going much slower', they reported enthusiastically.

'It can't be', I replied in disbelief. 'We haven't made any physical changes to your street yet. Nor have any other neighbourhoods signed the treaty'. But the residents insisted that speeds were down, so I investigated. And they were right, speeds had dropped. I needed to know why.

I discovered that prior to the street party, many residents did not even know their immediate neighbours. Most of the kids in the street had never met. At the street party new friendships were formed. The street party also changed the way the adults and kids related to their street. The street was no longer viewed as just a place for traffic. It was now seen as a legitimate place for play and socializing. So in the weeks after the party, the new social relationships and changed view of the street resulted in a dramatic increase in the number of kids playing on the sidewalk and adults standing in the street chatting. Put yourself in the shoes of a motorist driving down Henry Street. Last week there were no kids playing on the sidewalk. In fact, there was little sign of any life in the street. But now there were kids playing on the sidewalk and adults standing around talking. As a motorist, what would be your natural instinct? Without even thinking, you will slow down. Kids are unpredictable, and one may chase a ball out into the street. So you slow down, just in case. And natural curiosity means you just have to slow down to have a 'sticky beak' at the adults who are standing around talking. Who are they? What are they talking about? What is their story?

The increase in community activity in Henry Street had caused motorists to slow down without the motorists even being conscious that the new social activities in the street were seducing them into driving slower.

The speed of traffic on most streets is determined to a large extent by the degree to which the residents have psychologically retreated from their street.

At this point I had one of those 'aha' experiences. The speed of traffic on most streets is determined to a large extent by the degree to which the residents have psychologically retreated from their street. This means that working with people's perceptions of their street and creating social infrastructure may be more effective in slowing traffic than building speed bumps. Although I do believe that design still plays an important role and we will come to this later.

But moving the kids from the roadway to the sidewalk is like giving the motorist a permission slip to speed in the street!

If we understand how we lost our streets to traffic in the first place it suddenly makes sense why traffic speed is governed by the degree of psychological retreat by the residents. Picture in your mind a time in the past when kids played in the street and adults would stand in the middle of the street chatting. When a car came along a kid would call 'car' and they would stand aside to let the car pass. For the motorist, the constant expectation that there may be kids playing in the street, just around the corner, meant that they kept their speed down – just in case. Please note that the kids did not necessarily need to be playing in the street for the motorist to go slower. It was the constant expectation that there *might* be kids playing in the street, just around the corner. Now imagine that one irresponsible motorist goes down a street too fast and almost hits a child. The child's parent responds by telling their child it is too dangerous to play in the roadway and that they must play on the sidewalk instead. The other parents follow suite. But moving the kids from the roadway to the sidewalk is like giving the motorist a permission slip to speed in the street! Now you have probably worked out the rest of the story. Because traffic is now going faster, the adults tell the children to stop playing on the sidewalk and to play in the back yard or at the local park. This makes the driving environment even less risky and more predictable, so the drivers raise their speed. The parents respond by not allowing their kids to walk to their friends, the local park, or school. They drive them instead, reducing even further the number of people in the street and adding more traffic to other streets. Because the street is now not a very nice place to be, elderly people stop sitting out in the street, and people do not spend as much time gardening or sitting on

their front steps. This weakens the informal community network in the street and becomes an open invitation for motorists to see the street, not as a social space in which they must act as a guest, but as a space that is owned exclusively by them.

Grandad teaches his grandson how to kick the ball, and helps slow traffic as a bonus!

This not only caused traffic to slow in their street, it was the catalyst for an upsurge in the vitality of neighbourhood life.

My discovery in Henry Street – that speed is governed to a large extent by the degree of residents psychological retreat – led to a series of experiments in neighbourhoods in cities around the world. I worked with residents, like Anne Hausrauth in Boise, Idaho, to psychologically reclaim their street and move some of their everyday activities closer to the street. They reported that this not only caused traffic to slow in their street, it was the catalyst for an upsurge in the vitality of neighbourhood life.

Dear David,

I just wanted to fill you in on what my block has been doing since you left. On Veteran's Day, November 11, my husband and I threw a bunting American flag with the stripes cut to create streamers up onto a horizontal branch of a big tree so that it hung over the roadway. It looked great! My 85-year-old neighbour, whose wife died about 4 years ago, asked me how we got it up in the tree and then talked about his experience in Italy during World War Two. So, I started out focused on slowing traffic down and ended up allowing Mr McWhirter, my neighbour to enrich both of our Veteran's Day experiences. (I'm a pacifist and this was a very good experience for me as well.)

Then, that night we invited all of the 11 households on our block for ice-cream and to watch your video. Three other families came and we plotted! On Saturday, which was a gorgeous, warm day, we moved our old picnic table out from the back deck into the space where we normally park our car on the street. I started painting it bright red and soon had many helpers! The kids were so enthusiastic, I hauled out our kitchen table and had them paint it in the street.

After a while, I dragged a huge wicker rocking chair off our back balcony and set it up as the first street-reclaiming chair. It was perfect for the two six-year-olds to rock vigorously in when they weren't painting or doing art work with sidewalk chalk on our retaining wall next to the sidewalk. Shortly, Melissa, the 10-year-old had another chair out and was reading in the place where they normally park their car.

The reaction from motorists was wonderful! Regrettably, at various times all of us adults have shouted, "slow down" at someone driving too fast down our street and their reactions have been obscene gestures or scowls. This Saturday people slowed down and some of them asked us what the occasion was. There were a large number of bicyclists and people with strollers and almost everyone, including motorists, smiled at us – quite convincing evidence of the power of street reclaiming!

Sunday was an equally gorgeous day so I dragged our portable solar cooker off the back balcony and set it up across the street where neighbours normally park a car. It took 1 1/4 hour to bake solar brownies and we shared them with neighbour kids and bicyclists and walkers.

There are a lot more stories. Stay tuned and thank you so much!!! for your inspiration. You have given all of us on the 1800 block of N. 7th street hope and we're having such fun in the process! Unfortunately it is raining, finally, but we have great plans for Christmas lights across the street and I'm quite certain that I can make a lot of banners!

[Later communication] The really great thing is that here on this block, several families are taking ownership of the project; sharing magazine articles about Christmas decorations, beginning to buy /make interesting/bizarre adornments. Stay tuned and thanks again for getting us started. This is the most fun I've had in ages!!

Anne

Instant Street Reclaiming

I also organized more formal events that I called 'Instant Street Reclaimings'. I would go into a street and demonstrate how residents could help bring speeds down, starting with just the contents of a suitcase. I would start these events by observing how residents had retreated psychologically from their street, and then get the residents to reverse the retreat. This usually took anything from one hour to half a day.

Let me tell you about one such event in Massachusetts, run in a heavy traffic street with over 10,000 vehicles per day. It was a classic example of a street in which residents had totally retreated psychologically. The residents had suggested meeting at a small park nestled in the fork of a Y intersection. Only four residents initially showed up. The first thing that struck me was where they chose to meet – the spot in the centre of the park that was furthest from the traffic on either side. I also observed that all the seats in the park and all the activity zones were also located in the centre of the park. The edges of the park that fronted the street were barren of anything that would encourage human activity. So the first step in this Instant Street Reclaiming was to move our discussion to the sidewalk, right at the Y in the intersection. The four participants all commented how the traffic seemed to slow when we moved to the sidewalk. I then observed that there were no cars parked in the street. When I asked why not, the residents responded, 'Are you crazy. The traffic goes too fast. It is too dangerous'. So I explained that not having their cars parked in the street was an open invitation for the traffic to go fast. I convinced them to get their cars and park them right near where we were standing. I wanted to compress the 'activity zone' for major impact.

Parking the cars brought the traffic speed down further. So I then set up my Official Street Reclaiming Chair in a parking bay. The Street Reclaiming Chair is a brightly coloured throne and stage setting that folds out of a suitcase (see picture below). If traffic volumes are low I can often set up the Street Reclaiming Chair right in the middle of the street safely, but in this street, traffic volume and speed was still too high. You know instinctively what is safe and what is not and I never ask residents to do anything that is unsafe. Setting the chair up brought speeds down

The Official Street Reclaiming Chair that folds out of a suitcase.

significantly and also encouraged many residents to come out of their homes and ask what was happening. I invited these residents to go home and get their own chairs and join me. We got toys and put them on the side of the street. Each activity we added brought the speeds down. With each drop in speed we felt safer to inch the activities out into the roadway, which brought speeds down even further. Within an hour it was safe to let kids do chalk drawings in the street. One elderly gentleman asked me if he could draw a picture of his dead cat on the street. At no time during this process did we block traffic or close the street to traffic. This was a demonstration of how the social life of a street can calm traffic dramatically and how the withdrawal of that social life is an open invitation for traffic to go faster.

For me, these Instant Street Reclaiming events raised a serious question: 'What is happening in the heads of the motorists that causes them to slow down?'.

Even though the answer may seem obvious, I thought that articulating the answer could provide the key for better understanding how to use social activity and design to seduce motorists into going slower. In fact, articulating the answer did far more than I expected. It led me to a radical reappraisal of the methods engineers are currently using to make our neighbourhood streets 'safer'.

I concluded that there were three key factors that automatically change motorists 'head space' and cause them to slow down without them even being conscious that they are slowing down: intrigue, uncertainty and humour. These three act as 'mental speed bumps'.

I will tell a series of stories to show how each of these work. Understanding how these mental speed bumps work is absolutely vital to understanding why the Hans Monderman approach to design, and my approach to both design and social activity, calms drivers subconsciously. It also explains why Traffic Calming (as currently practiced) is a blunt instrument that in many cases can be counter-productive – calming traffic but enraging the motorist.

A child paints the street at an Instant Street Reclaiming.

Mental Speed Bump 1: Intrigue

I was on tour to publicize my book *Street Reclaiming*, my first tentative reporting of the lessons I had learned from the Henry Street experiment. I arrived at an afternoon public meeting in Boise, Idaho, to find three television news crews waiting on the steps of the hall. We were running very late. So I told them I would have to do a joint news conference rather than one-on-one interviews. But my host had other ideas. 'Get him to set up his Street Reclaiming Chair', he said to the reporters. I replied that we were already late, but he simply said, 'I will tell the people waiting inside that this is part of your presentation'.

So I set the chair up right in the middle of the intersection outside the hall, taking up about as much space as a mini-roundabout. Soon the traffic began to back up as each driver queued to ask me what was happening. The cue got longer if I took longer to answer their question. But there was something very un-American about this traffic queue – no one got angry. Instead there were waves, smiles, good humour and lots of banter. One driver even asked if I minded him joining me. 'Be my guest', I replied, not having a clue what he meant by joining me. He parked his car, went to the truck and took out a flute. He came over and began playing classical music and dancing around my chair. All this activity caused

The more mysterious the pieces of the puzzle, the greater our level of engagement in trying to guess the story.

people to come out of their houses. For some reason, the fact that I was in the centre of their street seemed to legitimize residents holding their conversations, not on the sidewalk, but right in the middle of the street. Kids brought out their bikes and pedal cars and began riding around in the street. And the motorists continued to queue patiently, waiting to ask, 'So what's going on here?'. The media thought we had staged this entire event, but it was completely spontaneous.

Why did the motorists queue patiently? Intrigue. When we are intrigued we are faced with a situation that does not make immediate sense. Why would someone be sitting in the middle of an intersection on a brightly coloured throne? Being curious creatures, we want to know what is happening and why it is happening. We want the full story. Our curiosity must be satisfied.

We all have a storyteller living in our heads. The storyteller derives great pleasure from gathering all the pieces of a puzzle and trying to create a picture from the disparate pieces. The more mysterious the pieces of the puzzle, the greater our level of engagement in trying to guess the story.

This insight about intrigue has had an important application for the Instant Street Reclaiming events that I organize. One of my cardinal rules has become 'No Signs'. Signs decapitate intrigue. Imagine if, when I set up my Street Reclaiming Chair in the Boise intersection, I had put up a sign saying 'Warning: Australian author deliberately holding up traffic'. I would have destroyed the intrigue factor. Intrigue only works as long as we allow the mystery and ambiguity to remain. The observer must be left unaided to unearth the story behind what they observe. In fact, intrigue is an irresistible challenge to the storyteller in the head of the motorist.

Intrigue only works as long as we allow the mystery and ambiguity to remain.

Masks increase the level of intrigue because they mask part of story.

Why did the motorists queue patiently at the Boise intersection? The storyteller in the head of each motorist had to know if the story they had constructed was remotely right.

When we are intrigued and in storyteller mode, we must observe the smallest details because it is often the smallest details that unlock the mystery of the 'what's the story?' puzzle. You can't observe minute details while driving fast. You must slow down, or even stop. The reason I developed a golden rule of no official signs for Instant Street Reclaiming events was that signs kill intrigue. Once the story has been told, the storyteller in the motorist's head is sated, and the 'driver' resumes control and they can get back to what they were doing before the storyteller became intrigued – speeding to some destination. The longer we can keep the person intrigued, the longer they will slow down. So the absence of signs helps bring speeds down, making it safe for us to be in the street in the first place.

This insight into the role of intrigue in reducing traffic speed has significant implications for the design of our streets. Standardized traffic control devices and signs do not require the storyteller in our head to be engaged. The story has already been told by an engineer. A speed bump says: 'slow down or be severely jolted!'. But there is a human story behind every speed bump and traffic control device, a story that has been lost in the telling. For example, imagine a street in which a child is knocked from their bike and killed. The residents do the only thing they know – lobby for traffic calming. The residents fight city hall for two years, and finally win, getting a series of speed bumps in their street. But the motorists driving down this street have absolutely no idea about the story behind

Signs kill intrigue. Standardized traffic control devices and signs do not require the storyteller in our head to be engaged.

the speed bumps. The only story they read is, 'Idiot engineer/residents forcing me to slow down!'. But what if the residents had known about the power of intrigue. What if they suspended a child's bike above the street, a bike being led by a seagull. On the bike is a flag that reads, 'Jane, may you ride forever'. Now the storyteller in the motorists' head is forced to be engaged and slow down to collect the clues. Why is there a child's bike suspended over the street? Why the seagull and sign: 'Jane, may you ride forever'? Ah, Jane must have been a child killed riding her bike in this street. How old was she? I wonder if she looked like my daughter when she was eight? How would I feel if it were my daughter that was killed? This suspended bike over the street tells a far more powerful story than a series of speed bumps.

Even a pedal car left in the middle of the street tells a more compelling story than a speed bump. There must be kids living in this street.

Why did they leave their pedal car there? Have they gone for afternoon tea? Will they come back? Ah, I remember when I use to ride my pedal car in the street. I got it for my sixth birthday.

Engineers (and remember I am not beating up on engineers) love standardization, which not only means that they tell the same story over and over, but the story behind the story is totally lost and debased.

Intrigue is one of those magic feelings that changes our perceptions of time.

Intrigue is one of those magic feelings that changes our perception of time. A good storyteller can keep us spellbound for hours. Time can stand still. The storyteller in our head can do the same. Therefore, when we intrigue motorists we engage their storyteller and change their relationship to time. They move from automated machine governed by the ticking clock in which seconds are dollars, to playful child absorbed in the never-ending now, where there are no limits and everything is possible. In fact, when we are in storytelling mode, the clock is a curse because it demands that we re-enter the boring world of the mundane. This is why the motorists at the Boise intersection queued patiently. They had been switched from motoring mode into storytelling mode. They were not held up in traffic. They were telling themselves a good yarn.

Before continuing, let me pre-empt a major objection to the mental speed bumps approach to taming traffic, particularly the removal of all traffic control devices. Many people have said, 'Ah, that will never work in Australia

Australians and North Americans are just as prone to becoming absorbed in a good yarn as Europeans.

or the USA because the drivers are more impatient and rude than they are in Europe'. Leaving aside for a moment the very subjective judgment that drivers in these countries are more impatient, this objection misses the key way in which mental speed bumps calm drivers subconsciously; they switch the driver persona off and the storytelling persona on. Australians and North Americans are just as prone to becoming absorbed in a good yarn as Europeans. My major proving ground for the power of mental speed bumps, as epitomized in the story above, has been the USA.

Let me tell one other story that underlines the power of intrigue to tame drivers subconsciously. When I first started doing Instant Street Reclaiming events, I would often find that residents were so angry with traffic that they would shake their fists and yell at the drivers. In the early days I used to instruct residents to unclench their fist and their teeth, and to smile and wave at the motorists. My reason was fairly simple. You can't expect motorists to act like a guest in your street if you are going to treat them as an enemy. But I soon found an extraordinary outcome when people stopped shaking their fist and waved instead. Without fail, the residents would exclaim: 'My goodness, they really do go much slower'. What was happening in the motorist's head? Well when you shake your fist and yell at someone, you don't need to slow down to work out the story. The message is as blunt as a speed bump. Thousands of years of evolutionary conditioning kicks in and tells the motorist: 'Enemy! Stop and fight, or flee quick!'. In fact, a closed fist does exactly the opposite to what the residents are actually requesting. It tells the motorist to speed up.

But when people smile and wave, there is no immediately obvious story. First we have to slow down enough to see if they are friends or acquaintances. If we do not immediately recognize their faces, then we must slow down even further to see if they might be someone we once met, but haven't seen for a long time. When we still do not recognize them the mystery deepens. Is this a special day I am not aware of? Maybe they mistook me for someone else? Or maybe this is an incredibly friendly neighbourhood? The storyteller in the motorist's head may stay engaged for some blocks. Meanwhile, the driver in their head has taken a back seat.

First we have to slow down enough to see if they are a friend or acquaintance.

Mental Speed Bump 2: Uncertainty

I have conducted dozens of Instant Street Reclaiming events in cities all over the world. We never close the street to traffic, put up barricades, or use official warning signs for these events. The rationale is quite simple. We are demonstrating how neighbourhood activity and car movement can coexist spontaneously in the same space. In the past, when kids played in the street, they did not have to put up official warning signs. The reason? Uncertainty forced motorists to slow down without them even being aware that they were slowing down.

Intrigue and uncertainty are twins. Uncertainty takes over where intrigue ends. Intrigue is the storyteller concerned about the present. Intrigue asks the question: 'What is the story behind what I am observing at this moment in time?'. Uncertainty is the storyteller concerned about the future. It asks the question: 'What happens next?'. For uncertainty, the story is only half told and it is not sure how the story may unfold. Those kids playing on the sidewalk, are they going to stay there or chase a ball out into the middle of the road? Those people standing having a conversation, are they about to step into the roadway or continue their conversation (or both)? Uncertainty, like intrigue, keeps us engaged with our immediate surroundings. We are reliant on the smallest details to

Uncertainty is the storyteller concerned about the future. It asks the question: 'What happens next?'.

give us a clue as to how the story may unfold.

In one city we had a dramatic illustration of how uncertainty helps to make a street safer and how removing that uncertainty makes a street less safe. The city engineer insisted that for the instant street reclaiming event we put 274 red traffic cones down the centre of the street and erect half a dozen official warning signs. Traffic would use one half the street and the residents would do the street reclaiming activities on the other half. It was without doubt the most dangerous street event I have ever conducted. The traffic devices told the motorists they could be certain of their space. The signs and cones were a covert promise of predictability and certainty. So the motorists speed down the corridor reserved as their exclusive space. Yet this promise of certainty and predictability was a totally false promise. Just a few metres from the speeding traffic were children playing with bikes and balls.

The signs and cones were a covert promise of predictability and certainty.

The engineer who insisted we put 274 traffic cones up the centre of the street was doing what planning professionals like to do: reduce uncertainty by placing boundaries on the potential stories that may unfold in space/time. The cones were an attempt to make the future more predictable for the motorists. Unfortunately it had an unforeseen consequence that was potentially catastrophic. By creating an illusion of certainty about the future, the engineer seduced motorists into driving faster. The cones masked the true level of risk and created a 'false sense of security'. This situation is being repeated in cities all around the world. A city will pass an ordinance banning street games in the name of 'safety'. They then erect signs saying 'No Ball Games'. The motorist reads this sign as a sign that their environment is more predictable, so they do what comes naturally

The more neighbourhoods that build the social life of their street, the greater the uncertainty that is created in the motorists mind even when there is no social activity in the street.

– speed up and reduce their level of vigilance. At the same time the city encourages children to walk to school. When one drops their ball and chases it into the street the motorist is in the wrong mental state to deal with it. Unwittingly the city has created a false sense of security. (I explain more about this in the chapter: *The Safety Paradox*).

When I explain to residents how intrigue and uncertainty automatically slow traffic, they often respond by saying: 'But it is impossible for us to keep social activity in our street all the time. Won't the motorists simply speed when we are not in the street?'. No. Earlier I explained the importance of 'expectation'. When children played in the centre of the street, motorists went slower because just around the corner there *might* be children playing in the street. This uncertainty caused them to drive slower. Sure, this expectation will not develop over night. But the more neighbourhoods that build the social life of their street, and the more prevalent this social life, the greater the uncertainty that is created in the motorists mind even when there is no social activity in the street.

There is also another kind of uncertainty that slows motorists automatically – uncertainty about the rules of engagement when we first enter someone else's space. When we first visit someone's house, we are uncertain about the rules of etiquette, so we absorb all the clues to try and decipher the rules of engagement. If we see a collection of shoes at the doorway, we assume we should take our shoes off. We look for clues as to which chair we should sit in, and whether we should be formal or informal. If we see a religious picture on the wall, we may conclude that swearing and dirty jokes will not be appropriate in this setting.

If there were a list of rules posted on the front door, then this uncertainty would be resolved and we would no longer have to be as vigilant or engaged with the immediate surroundings. Signs depersonalize a space, making it feel anonymous. Similarly, traffic signs depersonalize the street as socializing space. Ironically, the subtext of official signs and traffic control devices is that no one in particular owns a space, so motorist's no longer have to act like a guest.

Signs also treat motorists as idiots and potential troublemakers. Take, for example, the practice of putting a Keep Left sign (Keep Right in North America and Europe) on every concrete island in the centre of the street. If we really believe that motorists are so stupid they don't know which side of the island to drive then they should not have a licence. Treat people like an idiot and potential troublemaker, and they usually fulfil your expectations.

Signs depersonalize a space. But the presence of this elderly lady rehumanizes a street, bringing with her both intrigue and uncertainty.

Mental Speed Bump 3: Humour

I rely on a bicycle as my major form of transport. Sporadically in the past I have been the target of road rage. I have been run off the road several times, had things thrown at me, and once was punched and kicked. But for the past few years I have not had a single incidence of road rage. Has this been the result of road rage in general declining? No, it has been on the rise. So why have motorists suddenly stopped taking their aggression out on me?

I was in Canada at a conference and found a pair of red devil's horns that you can Velcro onto the side of your bike helmet (helmets are compulsory in Australia). Being mildly eccentric, I bought them. I arrived home, stuck them on my helmet, but didn't ride for about a week. Obviously, when you have your helmet on, you can't see the horns, so it is natural to forget that you are wearing them. The first day I wore my new horns I thought someone had put something magic in the Brisbane water supply while I had been away. People were smiling at me. Little kids would tap their parents on the shoulder, point, give a sheepish grin and sometimes wave. Instead of abusing me, motorists would wind their window down at the intersection and have a jocular conversation. Passengers would lean out the window as their car slowly inched past me

and say, 'Horny devil hey'. I was deeply puzzled as to what had triggered this incredible change in behaviour – until I remembered the horns on my helmet. They had somehow magically transformed the public space. And the reason I have not had another incidence of road rage? It is hard for people to be angry when they are laughing. There is something basic and universal about a smile or a laugh. It is one of the few forms of communication that transcends language and cultural barriers. Humour, therefore, humanizes public space, especially street spaces that have become anonymous and depersonalized.

Humour, like uncertainty, is a close relative of intrigue. Humour engages the storyteller by throwing it an unresolvable riddle. The logic of a helmet is that it is used to protect a cyclist's head from irresponsible motorists and/or accidents. But when the helmet suddenly sprouts devil's horns, there is no logical explanation. Our only human response, when faced with such an absurdity, is to smile and laugh.

Humour humanizes public space, especially street spaces that have become anonymous and depersonalized.

According to Edward de Bono, humour builds a new neuronal tract in our brain. Our brains are a self-organizing system. When you are born your brain is like a virgin landscape. Imagine that when you are just a toddler, an older sibling scratches you. Your brain tries to make sense of this event and forges a new path through you mental landscape. The number of potential pathways your brain could have chosen to explain this event is infinite, but for a range of reasons it chooses a particular path. The next time your sibling scratches you, your brain does not have to do as much work to interpret this event. It follows the same path it did last time. The more often your sibling repeats the scratching, the more entrenched this pathway becomes. Years latter, if a trusted friend hurts you, you will use the pathway already beaten into the mental landscape to interpret this event.

These pathways we create in our mental landscape are influenced by social and cultural norms, our environment and probably by our own genetic make up. When we are thinking 'rationally', incoming data travels these well-worn tracks without us even needing to think. But humour and the absurd jolt the incoming data onto a completely different track – a speed bump that jolts you so bad you end up on a different street! The story is developing in a very logical manner when, wham, you are no longer on the same track of logic. In finding your way back to the main track, you are forced to make a new neuronal tract between the sidetrack you found yourself on and the main track you were on previously. Suddenly you find yourself on a new mental adventure, exploring territory you did not even know existed. Finding your way back to the main track may only take a split second, or it may take months. Regardless of how long the adventure takes, building this new neural track in our brains releases certain chemicals that make us feel more alive. We laugh, chuckle and savour the moment. We want to hang onto that moment and feeling as long as we possibly can. We are in the world of exploring new territory, a world where time stands still.

Taking humour into the public realm is to offer an unconditional gift to whoever wishes to take it. When I see people smiling at my devil's horns, I often wonder how I have affected their day. How long does their elevated mood last? Are they less likely to get mad with other motorists? Do they go to work and treat their fellow workers or customers a little better? Are they more generous and giving?

Taking humour into the public realm is to offer an unconditional gift to whoever wishes to take it.

I was once in London having lunch at a café. Opposite me sat a woman in her early sixties with bright red hair. I said to my companion: 'I wish I had the guts to do something like that'. When I got back to Australia I kept thinking about this woman and how brave she was. I put my toe in the water by getting a couple of purple streaks put in my hair. Then I went all out and dyed the whole lot purple. I couldn't believe the effect this had on other people. Whereas I could walk a dozen blocks in my neighbourhood and not have a single person say hello, now I would have as many as five conversations in a single block. Some of these were deep conversations about grabbing life by the horns and stepping outside one's comfort zone. And it was an absolute delight to watch the face of kids in the supermarket as they pulled at their parent's arm and giggled while they pointed in my direction. As a bonus my own creativity blossomed.

I often think of that lady with the red hair. Did she have any idea of the gift she had handed me? Did she know she had given me the courage to break through to a new level of self-confidence and creativity? Did she have any idea that I had multiplied that gift and passed it on to hundreds of others? Did she have any idea that she had helped humanize the streets in my neighbourhood? And how many other people had she inspired that day while she sat drinking coffee? And how far had these people spread that gift? Did she have any idea that as she sat in that café drinking her coffee and reading a book that she was changing the world, not only in London, but also in Australia?

Ah, and you thought the only way to create great public spaces and tame traffic was through design.

Kangaroos in Copenhagen

Ewa Bialecka from Poland won an international ideas competition by proposing that bouncing pads (like mini-trampolines) be installed in the sidewalks of Copenhagen. She observed that adults move in straight lines and in the horizontal plane only. But people love to explore the vertical plane by jumping to explore space above them or getting down on their haunches to explore the space below them. If adults explored the vertical plane by jumping on bouncing pads, they would defy the dictates of reason, and enter the timeless world of play. As Ewa said in her submission, 'While you are up in the air, everything changes. People start to smile at each other'.

While you are up in the air, everything changes.

Drawings from Ewa's submission.

Hans surveys a major intersection that has had all the traffic control devices removed.

A Dutch Engineer Straddles Paradoxical Worlds

Jodi, my 21-year-old daughter, rang me quite concerned. 'Dad, there was this guy on TV this morning and he has stolen all your ideas'.

After much detective work, I discovered the person she referred to was Ben Hamilton Baillie. Ben is a British architect turned street designer who went to the Netherlands to research the woonerf (an early forerunner of what latter became known as 'traffic calming'). During his research, Ben met an engineer by the name of Hans Monderman who provided a surprising twist to Ben's research. Hans was removing traffic calming devices while the rest of the world was putting more in. In fact he was removing traffic lights, stop signs and all official signage. After reading Ben's research paper I decided I just had to meet this Dutch engineer.

Hans suggested I catch the train from Amsterdam and meet him at the Utrecht railway station, and from there attend a conference presentation he was giving. In the afternoon we would tour some of the villages he had rebuilt. Hans' conference presentation provided a compass and map for me to understand what I would see that afternoon.

Hans explained how the engineering profession has been through

Hans was removing traffic calming devices while the rest of the world was putting more in.

Hans explained that his approach is radically different to these two historical approaches of isolation and accommodation.

two major approaches to dealing with traffic in villages and cities. Stage one he called 'isolation'. Traffic was dealt with in complete isolation from the impacts on people's living environments, what he called the social world. In the isolation phase, the only concern for engineers and planners was creating an efficient traffic system, efficiency being measured in the very narrow terms of a system that moved the maximum number of vehicles possible. How this impacted on the social life of the neighbourhood, village or city was of little concern.

In the late '60s and early '70s there was a reaction as people began feeling that the social life of the community was paying too high a price for all this increased mobility. The Dutch, with their strong cycling and pro-public-space traditions, led this revolution and helped usher in the second approach to traffic which Hans called 'accommodation'. In this phase, engineers and planners tried to re-engineer streets to accommodate both the traffic functions and the social functions. The woonerf gave priority to the social functions and created physical impediments to traffic going fast. The woonerf was very expensive because the entire street was rebuilt as a 'living yard', often with play areas for children and places to sit and chat. When other countries copied the woonerf, they found it too expensive so created a poor man's version, traffic calming. This involved putting in impediments to the traffic going fast (speed bumps and chicanes) but not the devices to facilitate the social life of the street such as play equipment.

Hans explained that his approach is radically different to these two historical approaches of isolation and accommodation. He calls the third approach 'accepting' – accepting that traffic is a legitimate part of the social life of the street, but not modifying the social world of the street to accommodate the traffic. In this approach the traffic must accommodate itself to the social life of the street, not vice versa.

For Hans there are two different worlds – the traffic world and the social world. In the traditional walled city, the city gates marked the transition point between the highway (traffic world) and the social world of the settlement. As you crossed the threshold, you changed from traveller into guest. Hans puts up a slide that shows how these two worlds are the inverse of each other. The traffic world is a predictable, uniform world which is highly governed by rules and regulations. The social world is unpredictable, full of diversity and democratic. Now Hans, the conservative Dutch traffic engineer who owns a racing green SAAB, believes

TRAFFIC WORLD	SOCIAL WORLD
Uniform	Diverse
Predictable	Unpredictable
Planned	Spontaneous
Compulsory	Voluntary
Anonymous	Personal
Vehicle Oriented	People Oriented
Technical Oriented	Relationship Oriented
Government Oriented	Community Oriented
Avoids conflict	Embraces conflict
Speed Oriented	Savors the moment

The social world is unpredictable, full of diversity and democratic.

passionately in the traffic world. He loves freeways between cities and I was shocked later in the day to hear him say that there is no limit to how much traffic we can move between cities by properly designing the traffic world. For him, traditional traffic engineering works wonderfully well in the traffic world. But the moment we enter a village or city we cross the threshold from traffic world into the social world. Here the motorist is welcomed as a guest in the social world, but they can no longer behave as they did in the traffic world. Instead they must become part of the social world where the rules of engagement are the absolute inverse of what they were in the traffic world.

For things to run smoothly in the traffic world, everything must be predictable as possible. But in the social world there has to be a balance between the predictable and the spontaneous and unplanned. I have written extensively in my previous books about how the quality of neighbourhood life is dependent almost exclusively on spontaneous and unpredictable 'exchanges'. While walking to the corner store we stop for a conversation with the elderly people sitting on the seat in the shade of the tree – a spontaneous exchange. We see a notice in a shop window advertising dance classes – a spontaneous exchange. We see someone eating an ice-cream and our mouth starts watering so we look for the shop

The vulnerable in our communities (the elderly, children, youth) are highly dependent on spontaneous exchanges as their means of participating in community life.

Traffic signs and traffic devices create their own frenetic pace.

where they bought it – a spontaneous economic exchange. The creative and economic life of the city are highly dependent on the spontaneous. At the conference, Hans had put up a slide showing how the values in the traffic world are the absolute inverse of those in the social world. He explained further: 'In the traffic world there are always simple solutions – more exams, more rules, more police, more regulations, more lanes, more signs. But in the social world things are not this simple'.

For Hans, the use of traffic control devices in the traffic world is appropriate and even essential. But in the social world they confuse the motorist because the motorist is not sure which world they are really in. We do not put up signs in our lounge room saying, 'Don't spit on the floor'. Such a sign is inappropriate for the context.

In the afternoon, as we drove through villages that had not yet been treated with Hans' radical approach, Hans would point to a sign indicating a bend in the street or some other traffic oriented device and ask rhetorically, 'Am I part of the traffic world or part of the social world? Please Mr. Engineer, tell me because I am confused'. After driving through the

first village in which all the traffic control devices had been removed, I experienced first hand what he was saying. There was a palpable sense of calmness and feeling of 'being at home' in these spaces. Traffic signs and traffic devices create their own frenetic pace. Your eyes dart from one sign to the next, constantly in motion. Everything is demanding an instant response. Stop. Go. Hurry. Don't park here. Park here, but not too long. Curve ahead. Kids ahead. Slow down. Speed up. This lane, not that one. Act now!! It was impossible for me to even begin to imagine how much calmer a street environment feels with all these demands for instant attention and action gone. You were left to savour the surroundings, at your leisure – to observe what was really happening in the social world around you. It literally freed you to connect with the social environment and become a part of it.

After leaving one of these villages we came to a crossroads and Hans said, 'And now we are crossing the threshold back into the traffic world'. And there it was. Dozens of traffic signs saying do this and don't do that. Traffic lights and white lines on the road to tell us exactly where to drive. A regulated, non-spontaneous world where time and conforming are all important – the inverse of everything we had valued while driving in the social world. Hans believes that the traffic world and social world should be very discrete areas with the transition zone between the two as small and sharp as possible. (I will return to this as a specific problem to be dealt with in 'modern' cities.)

The engineer in Hans Monderman believes we can only ask motorists to be human and not a motorist for so long. In the morning presentation he put up a chart of how long he thinks people are prepared to drive at certain speeds. In Hans' opinion, the length of time motorists are prepared to drive at human-scale speed means that villages and neighbourhoods should be no larger than two kilometres square. (Later he challenged his own thinking on this and I shall come to that part of the story soon.)

For now, let's return to the distinction between the old approach of accommodation – epitomized in traffic calming – and the Hans Monderman approach of acceptance. Hans explains that with acceptance,

The major intersection in Oosterwolde which has been converted into a town square.
All traffic control devices have been removed, even the lines to denote parking bays.

motorists are accepted into the social world, but the social world is not adapted for the motorists. For Hans the design challenge is: 'How do I make the motorist a social being rather than a motorist when they are driving in the social world?'. For him, it is the surroundings that tell the story of whether you should act as motorist or social being. Signs and traffic control devices (including traffic calming devices) destroy the social context. He argues that one of the strongest forms of communication in the social world is eye contact. To make motorists part of the social world, Hans believes his primary design challenge is to force motorists into eye contact with the other users of the space. Traffic control devices remove the need to make eye contact. 'If there is nothing to tell the motorist how to act, they will look to others in the space for help'.

Hans believes his primary design challenge is to force motorists into eye contact with the other users of the space.

I stood in a town square and watched his theory at work. The town square was the major intersection in the village. There were no traffic lights, no roundabout, no lane markings and no stop signs. It was utterly unclear where cars should drive or even park, where pedestrians and cyclists should walk or ride, what was public space for sitting, talking, playing or selling merchandise. Users of the space were clearly using eye contact to negotiate their way through the square. But it was also clear that informal rules of behaviour had been negotiated among the locals. A young female cyclist sped through the space, obviously certain that a certain protocol would be followed.

It is here that we are exposed to the very heart of what both Hans and I have been working on. In the words of Hans: 'If you want motorists to behave as if they are in a village, then build a village'. As he explained to me, this is not a case of simply ripping out all the traffic control devices. It

'If you want motorists to behave as if they are in a village, then build a village'.

is a case of every detail of the environment telling a consistent story. For example, if the residents treat their own street as a traffic corridor rather than as part of their social world, then the environment will still send mixed messages, even if every traffic control device has been removed.

'I don't try to solve traffic problems', Hans tells me as we stand examining yet another major intersection that has had the traffic lights removed and turned into a traditional village square. 'I concentrate on the quality of public space. When you see traffic problems as a traffic problem you will only ever get traffic solutions'. As Hans sees it, traffic per se is not the problem. The real problem is that motorists feel divorced and isolated from their social surroundings. The design signals confuse the motorists about how they should behave in the space. Are they part of the traffic world or part of the social world? His challenge is to un-confuse the motorist by providing clear signals and to integrate them into the social world. At one level this has nothing to do with using engineering devices that force the motorist to behave appropriately (the traditional traffic calming approach). In fact engineering devices such as speed bumps simply reinforce the mixed messages.

How it all began

Hans' father was a teacher. As a child he moved from town to town and he felt like he never truly belonged to any one community. Hans trained as a civil engineer then later as a traffic engineer. As a traffic engineer his specialty was safety. For him safety had become a very technical field that completely ignored the human factors. Hans became fascinated with how humans relate to their physical surroundings and how the surroundings influence perceptions and people's state of mind.

Because of his childhood and his professional experience, Hans has always been interested in the 'borderlands'. As we cruised down a freeway, I explained to him my belief that all creativity and innovation happens in the borderlands. For the past 25 years, Hans has been employed as a 'free agent' to work across all levels of government on traffic issues. He believes this has been an important ingredient in his developing a new understanding of motorist behaviour as he has been forced to live in the borderlands between government departments. In addition, he has had no money to spend on projects. This means he must use the strength of

'When you see traffic problems as a traffic problem you will only ever get traffic solutions'.

*The main street of Oudehaske, where it all began in 1984. Traffic Calming was
replaced with traditional brick road, low curb and intimate street lighting.*

his argument – not the threat of withholding funding – as his means of exercising his authority. In fact he says he hates money because it kills innovation.

Up until 1984, Hans was a great believer in traffic calming – re-engineering roads to slow traffic. But in 1984 he was asked to redesign the main streets of Oudehaske. It was at this time that those who paid his salary turned against traditional traffic calming. This meant that all the major tools in his engineering tool kit had been suddenly taken away from him. He had no idea what to do, other than to perhaps make the streets fit more sympathetically with the village. So he employed some design consultants and asked them to help him design the streets more in harmony with a traditional village. Hans did not believe in the resultant design. He didn't think it would really work because there were no overt elements to stop people speeding. Because his hands were tied politically, he decided to proceed with the design anyway.

When the design was finished and they did the first speed checks, Hans was astonished. 'When we do a traditional traffic calming with speed bumps we typically expect about a 10% drop in speed. But with no disincentives, the speed was down by almost 50% – down from 57 km/h to under 30 km/h. I could not believe my eyes. All we had done was make the village look more like a village'.

Hans started applying this lesson to other villages and today there are over 30 villages that have simply been 'villagafied'. His approach has now been called 'Shared Space' and the European Union is funding 5 demonstration projects across Europe. Hans is also acting as a consultant to about another 17 projects.

'All we had done was make the village look more like a village'.

'Why are planners and engineers so frightened of conflict?'.

One of the things I found refreshing about Hans was his lack of fundamentalist zeal for his own insights. 'As soon as I have discovered one thing, I am wondering what I will learn next, and how this may change the way I see the world today'. This attitude comes through in an important part of Hans' design work. We stood at the major intersection in Oosterwolde that had been converted into a town square. Hans explained to me, 'When I designed it people asked, 'But where will the cars park?' I replied, 'I don't care, that is not my problem'. So they said, 'What if people park inappropriately'? And I replied: 'Well if the village has a problem with where people are parking, let the village sort it out. It is not my job to try and forecast every potential problem the village may have in the future and try to pre-empt what may or may not be a problem through design". Hans continued, 'Why are planners and engineers so frightened of conflict? Conflict is a normal part of the democratic process in the social world. When we try to eliminate conflict by over-regulating physical design we actually weaken the evolution of a robust and vibrant social world'.

For Hans, the design of space can either weaken or strengthen the democratic process. Over-regulated space takes away the need for people to negotiate directly with their neighbours. This partly explains what Hans means when he says his job is not solving traffic problems but rather helping to create a village out of the village. The physical design of space has an immediate impact on the way people relate to each other. By forcing eye contact, Hans is putting people in direct communication with each other.

Hans' flexibility came through in another discussion we had about time. He thinks that understanding how humans perceive time may provide the next big breakthrough in his thinking. 'Our perceptions of time are determined by our context', he explained. 'If you are waiting for the dentist every second seems like an eternity. By contrast, after an evening of good food, wine and conversation we ask where the time went. In the traffic world time is everything. The instrument panel in front of us tells us how fast we are going, how far we have travelled and how much energy we have consumed. This is a world in which everything is measured in quantity. But in the social world, time moves at a gentler pace and is relative to the quality of experience. The greater the quality of experience, the slower time moves. It can even stand still'.

Moving people into storytelling mode changes their perceptions of time.

One can hypothesize that if we make motorists feel part of the social world, their perceptions of time will change. It was this discussion that stimulated me to explore how moving people into storytelling mode changes their perceptions of time. It led to my developing the whole notion of Mental Speed Bumps. One can further hypothesize that the greater the quality of this connection to the social world, the greater the motorist's natural instincts to travel slower to absorb the experience. Importantly, it also suggests that motorists may well tolerate driving at slower speeds for much longer, maybe even breaking Hans' golden rule that motorists will only tolerate travelling at certain speeds for so long. This is because their perceptions of how long they have been driving slowly will be determined by the quality of the context.

For Hans, one of the important implications of this insight about time is that keeping motorists moving, rather than stop-starting, is important in determining their perceptions about how long a journey is taking. 'People will tolerate lower speeds as long as they keep moving'. I related to him how one of my friends would rather add five minutes to her journey time driving through back streets than to be stuck in traffic. Hans believes that this goal of keeping traffic moving is just one further argument for reducing traffic control devices.

Hans Monderman freely admits that his specific design approaches may not translate well into other contexts. Most of his work has been in rural Dutch villages. And I agree that his design approach needs significant contextualizing, particularly for Australian, North American and UK cities. I give some clues as to how I think this may unfold later in the book. However, what I think is important about Hans' work is the theoretical base he has developed and the fact that he has tested this theoretical base in a real-world design context.

PART 2

Reflection and Application

Traffic: A Social Problem, Not A Design Problem

Whether you live in a Dutch village or a large sprawling North American city, there are a number of conceptual bridges to be crossed before I can discuss how you can tame the traffic in your neighbourhood and city.

A mental speed bump for residents

Our community was outraged that authorities would even consider turning the main arterial through our neighbourhood into a de facto highway. According to the 'experts', traffic growth projections demanded it be widened. But where was all this traffic growth coming from? From people like my neighbour who drove less than one and a half blocks every morning to pick up the paper and milk. From people like me who drove their kids to school. From people like me who drove their car to public meetings to protest against a road being widened! We were the traffic we loathed.

So I argued that our community had no right to fight the road widening unless we did something about our own car use. I went out and bought a bicycle.

Asking your city to spend lots of money on forcing you and your neighbours to drive slower seems like a huge waste of your hard earned cash.

Let me be frank. Traffic is first and foremost a community problem and residents have no right expecting politicians, engineers and planning professionals to fix it for them. Hold on to your hats. I will have something to say to the politicians, engineers and planning professionals in a moment.

I have worked in neighbourhood after neighbourhood where residents were asking the city to spend large sums of money to slow down one of their neighbours. I once chaired a meeting of residents that were asking the city to spend $250,000 to slow speeding motorists. When I asked how many motorists were causing the problem, an elderly gentleman said, 'Five, and I can show you were everyone of them lives'. I quickly did the maths. 'You want the city to spend $50,000 of your hard earned cash on each of these individuals to get them to slow down? Wouldn't you be better knocking on their door and asking them what you would need to pay them in order for them to behave? I bet they will do it for a lot less than $50,000!'.

Asking your city to spend lots of money on forcing you and your neighbours to drive slower and less often seems like a huge waste of your hard earned cash – especially when you could get the same result, at absolutely no cost, by simply shaking hands with your neighbour and agreeing that you will all act like a guest in each other's neighbourhoods. The solution to traffic problems in neighbourhoods is not more speed bumps. The solution is an outbreak of civility that slows our rampant individualism. And that is a cultural challenge, not a physical design challenge.

The solution is an outbreak of civility that slows our rampant individualism. And that is a cultural challenge, not a physical design challenge.

Crossing the critical threshold – the tipping point

Ask many parents why they drive their kids to school and they'll tell you that the streets are too dangerous because of all the traffic – too many parents driving their kids to school. Or they are worried about stranger danger – caused by the fact that since nobody walks these days, there is no one in the street to watch out for their children. This is a vicious cycle that feeds on itself – a kind of social chain reaction that can result in civic meltdown. But this chain reaction is not automatically set off when the first parent decides to drive their child to school. Nor when the second parent decides to drive their child. However, there comes a point, a critical threshold, a 'tipping point', where just one more parent making this decision to drive their child sets off the downward spiral.

Crossing the critical threshold is a community problem that can only be addressed if the entire community finds a way to arrest and reverse the downward spiral.

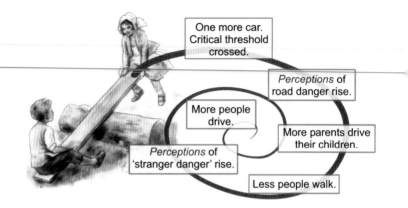

Now, who is responsible for the system crossing this critical threshold? The first parent who drove or the parent who was the last straw to break the camel's back? Neither. Crossing the critical threshold is a community problem that can only be addressed if the entire community finds a way to arrest and reverse the downward spiral.

We choose to live in villages or cities (rather than on our own in a cave) because living with other people is a cooperative enterprise in which everyone wins – everyone gives something to the enterprise and everyone gets back more than they gave. But sometimes the opposite is also true. We can take certain liberties (such as using public roads to drive a private vehicle) and end up with everyone losing, even when the liberty taken is legitimate. This is what happens with school and neighbourhood traffic. Up to a certain point, taking the liberty of using a car on public roads does not destroy other people's quality of life. But as we approach the tipping point, there are diminishing returns on the liberty taken, for those taking the liberty and for those whose lives are being impacted by increased traffic. When we cross the threshold, everyone loses, even those taking the liberty. Traffic is not a problem in a community until just before the tipping point and it is at this moment that the community must say to itself, 'We have to figure out a way to share this resource called liberty so that we are all winners and not losers'.

If the community has already crossed the critical threshold (as most have) then the community must figure out a way of sharing the liberty in a way that makes everyone a winner again. This may mean making some changes to our physical environment, but first and foremost it is about finding more creative ways of relating to each other as a community.

First and foremost it is about finding more creative ways of us relating to each other.

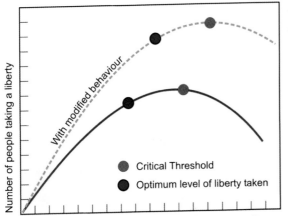

As more and more people take a liberty (like driving on public roads) we cross a threshold in which everyone loses. By modifying our behaviour, we can stave off this critical threshold and increase the benefits that accrue to everyone.

Number of people taking a liberty

With modified behaviour

⬤ Critical Threshold

⬤ Optimum level of liberty taken

Benefits that accrue to individuals and total community

*In community
after community
I see the 'politics
of blame' at work.
It is the other
drivers who are
destroying our
quality of life.*

This means making changes to our behaviour. For instance, it may mean everyone agreeing to drive slower in each other's neighbourhood so that the negative impacts of the traffic on neighbourhoods is lessened, thereby staving off the point at which we cross the critical threshold.

When I said that we have no right to ask politicians, engineers and design professionals to fix the traffic problems for us I meant that we are asking them to do something that is impossible. It is like an alcoholic asking a professional counsellor to fix their drinking problem for them so they have more time to get on with drinking. The alcoholic must take active steps to fix their own problem because it is their problem. Sure, they may ask a professional to help them kick their habit, but it remains their problem, not the professional's problem. If as a community we have crossed the tipping point (and most communities have) then the first step in addressing this issue is for us to take responsibility as a total community. There is nothing the engineer can do if we are not willing to look at our own behaviour and how it may have contributed to the larger community crossing the tipping point.

In community after community I see the 'politics of blame' at work. It is the *other* drivers who are destroying our quality of life. Somehow our driving does not effect any one's quality of life. It is the city who has failed to make the other drivers behave themselves. Very few communities have got to the point of saying, 'You know, I am both a motorist and a resident. It is not appropriate for me to demand unfettered freedom for myself when I am a motorist, but demand that restrictions be put on other motorists so that I have a better life as a resident. I must find a way to better balance the contradictory needs that I have as a motorist and a resident. Only then do I have the moral right to ask others to modify their behaviour'.

I am sorry I have had to be as blunt as a speed bump. But the old method of asking the government to solve the traffic problems for us is only making matters worse. If we make this conceptual leap, that traffic is, first and foremost, a social and community issue, the solutions become incredibly simple, cheaper and a hell of a lot more fun!

A jolt for city officials

So do my harsh words to the community let decision-makers and planning professionals off the hook? Not at all. Unwittingly, decision-makers and planning professionals have aided and abetted residents in playing the 'politics of blame' by taking responsibility for solving traffic problems for the community. I say 'unwittingly' because the planning professionals and decision makers have laboured under a false assumption that traffic issues (in the neighbourhood context) are primarily a design problem that can be fixed by changing the physical design of space.

Before I continue, it is important to understand that this book is dealing with traffic in the neighbourhood context – not freeway or high-way traffic. The central thesis of this book is that, in the neighbourhood context, traffic must be dealt with first and foremost as a social problem, and that design must be integrated into an understanding of sociology and psychology. This leads to a radical new approach to calming traffic in the neighbourhood context which combines social programs with a new approach to physical design.

I want to honour, in advance, those policy-makers, engineers and

Unwittingly, decision-makers and planning professionals have aided and abetted residents in playing the 'politics of blame'.

Looking at traffic through the prism of your total life experience will tear down the artificial walls that box in your thinking.

planning professionals who are willing to blaze a trail to a better future. This will take much courage since it will require you to let go of some longstanding practices and conventional wisdom. And it will require you to greatly expand the borders of your professional world.

There is one thing you may try that I think will make your journey a little more comfortable. Take off your 'decision maker' or 'design professional' hat. Instead put on your 'wise elder' hat and bring your total life experience to the table. Think like a parent, a motorist, a resident, a pedestrian, a cyclist, a citizen, and a child. Think of the things you enjoy in life or feel passionate about: reading novels, watching movies, eating at outdoor cafés, people-watching, music, or dancing. All breakthroughs in a particular discipline come when the frame of reference for the discipline is shifted. Looking at traffic through the prism of your total life experience will tear down the artificial walls that box in your thinking.

Creating borderlands

In 1996 I was invited to speak to a select group of Edinburgh's top bureaucrats over dinner. After dinner, David Begg, who was then in charge of Edinburgh's transportation, turned and asked me what was the secret of my creativity. I didn't have the foggiest idea. In fact I was rather surprised by his question. I had never thought of myself as 'creative'. But there was a nagging thought in the back of my mind that, if I was creative, it had something to do with my marginal experiences as a child.

In the '50s and '60s, when I was growing up, my father was an itinerant gospel preacher in the Assemblies of God, an extremely marginal Pentecostal church. Because my dad constantly moved, I attended 26 different schools, mostly in the first few years of my schooling. I was the target of school bullies almost every day of my school existence because I was always the new kid on the block and my dad was one of those people who 'walked on the ceiling'. I even had to take notes to school excusing me from folk dancing, because this would have aroused too much sensual desire. So I had to sit in the classroom alone, watching the kids below enjoying one of the few respites from the boring classes. My sitting alone in the classroom while the rest of the class danced outside is a metaphor for the borderlands – the space where irreconcilable worlds

Where my marginal experiences as a child the tidal mudflats of my creativity?

collide. My parents were deeply anti-intellectual, but here I was, part of a secular education system, yet anything but part of it. But neither was I really part of the fringe religious group to which I belonged. My father considered himself to be an outsider, a fringe-dweller in the Assemblies of God. So our family was on the fringe of the fringe – the ultimate in marginal territory. I did not know what it was to have a real friend until I turned 13 years of age.

David Begg's questions stirred my curiosity about the nature of creativity. I was thinking about my childhood experiences as I rode my bike to the State Library of Queensland to start my search for answers. Suddenly the penny dropped. I knew from my science classes at school (I loved science, even though a lot of it went against my religious beliefs) that one of the laws governing creativity in nature is the law of the borderlands: all creativity happens at the meeting point of two or more worlds. In nature, the most productive regions for evolving new life is where ecosystems meet and overlap, the ecotones: for example tidal mud flats where the sea meets land, a space which is neither sea nor land but both, an ambiguous territory where paradoxical worlds share the same space. I began to wonder, as I chained my bike to a post outside the library, whether my marginal experiences as a child were indeed the tidal mudflats of my creativity.

In the library I stumbled on the book *The Act of Creation* by Arthur Koestler. Koestler believes that humour is one of humanity's most primary and early creative acts. Humour is based on crashing two worlds of logic into each other. The meeting of these two previously unrelated worlds is a kind of marginal territory, a highly creative zone. Humans developed their ability for humour long before language was invented. Impersonating someone else in the tribe, maybe with a slight exaggeration, produced a rather nice bodily reaction – laughter. When people impersonate each other, they become two people at once – themselves and the person they impersonate. They become a borderland between the two. As humans developed language and other communication skills, our ability to tell stories and place ourselves in imaginary worlds blossomed. Storytelling remains a highly creative edge territory for the mind because the stories become the meeting place for separate worlds. And all good stories contain an irresolvable tension between paradoxical worlds: good versus evil; personal security versus self-sacrifice; immediate gratification versus long-term benefits; life versus death. This story itself encapsulates the borderlands, the clash of these irresolvable paradoxes.

Efficiency and richness of experience

Our modern cities were built on an assumption that cities would be more efficient if spaces had a clearly defined, rationalized function. Streets are for moving cars and parks are where children play. If you mix these two functions in the same space the space becomes less efficient. But this is only true if you look at the street

Cities are an invention to maximize exchanges and minimize travel.

in isolation from the city as a whole and if you only consider the movement function of the street and not its social function. If you look at the city as a total system, then the exact opposite is true.

In my previous books, I argued that cities are 'an invention to maximize exchanges and minimize travel'. These exchanges are economic, social, cultural, and personal. They range from a hug from a friend to drinking coffee alone and people-watching. The city deliberately concentrates a wide diversity of exchange opportunities into a bounded area in order to increase the efficiency with which these exchanges are transacted. The further these exchange opportunities are scattered, the further we must travel for each one, therefore the fewer we can enjoy.

Cities, like the internal space of buildings, are composed of two basic types of space – exchange spaces where exchanges are transacted and movement space for getting to the exchange spaces. Ancient city builders quickly realized that the more of the city given over to movement space, the less efficient the city became at performing its most basic function, facilitating exchange. The same is true for the internal space of a house. Rooms are where exchanges are transacted and the corridors are the spaces that get us to the rooms. Popular wisdom has it that corridors are a waste of space. To minimize corridor space, architects create 'dual purpose space' – that is, the room is used for both exchange and movement. At one moment of time the room can be used for an intimate conversation, at another moment it can be used to gain access to other rooms in the house. Early city builders used this same logic. Streets were 'outdoor living rooms' in which a wide range of economic, social and cultural exchanges could be transacted. But they were also used as movement space for getting to other exchange spaces in the city. Streets became the borderlands of the city, the tidal mudflats in which movement and exchange came together. And a new type of exchange evolved in this marginal territory – the spontaneous exchange. These spontaneous exchanges are what I have called 'exchanges for free'. They are a bonus we get while travelling for a planned exchange. And yet these spontaneous exchanges are often of much higher value to us than the original purpose for which we began the journey. With planned exchanges, we can only plan to access that which we already know. The spontaneous exchanges open up worlds we don't even know exist. They have a creative potential which is much higher than the planned exchange.

Streets became the borderlands of the city, the tidal mudflats in which movement and exchange came together.

By giving space a single, rationalized function, modern planners made the city less efficient.

By giving space a single, rationalized function, modern planners made the city less efficient because it dramatically reduced the number of spontaneous exchanges that could be transacted. It also made the city a much less stimulating place to be. The decrease in efficiency put more traffic on the streets and the decrease in mental stimulation made the motorists drive faster.

Earlier I explained how the brain is a self-organizing system. Data coming into the brain tends to choose a pathway through the brain that has been created for it by previous incoming data. I explained how humour jolts us onto a new path and we are forced to find our way back to the more familiar pathway. The borderlands work in much the same way to humour in breaking us out of our automated responses. Changing the analogy, we all have an 'automated secretary' in our brain that takes the incoming data and files it into pre-determined categories. (These 'categories' are completely arbitrary, much as the pathway through the bush is completely arbitrary and established through use over time.) When

Letting competing spaces overlap makes for a more compact and efficient city. The borderlands, created by overlapping functions, are 'denser', richer in colour and more mentally stimulating.

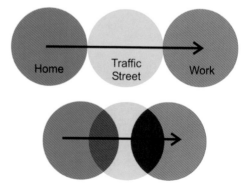

we enter the borderlands, the incoming data no longer fits within the existing categories. 'Damn it', says the subconscious brain, 'Is this private space or public space? Well it seems to be both. But it can't be. But it is'. Because the subconscious has no way of filing this information, it passes the problem over to the conscious part of the brain.

If we are travelling through a space that has been highly rationalized, the 'story' is mono-dimensional, flat, and over-familiar. But the borderlands are 'denser'. They are packed with intrigue, uncertainty, and humour. The storyteller in our head is automatically engaged.

Making physical borderlands reflect mental borderlands

The brain of every human contains paradoxical personas. We all have an 'explorer' or 'traveller' in our heads that has its roots in the hunter-gatherer phase of our evolution. The explorer needs to be able to move in order to survive, grow, and be nourished. However, every one of us also has a 'homebody' persona in our heads. The homebody has its genesis in the gardener phase of our evolution when we learnt the value of growing a garden, putting our hands in the soil and feeling rooted to one spot. The homebody needs to stay still in order to survive, grow and be nourished. These two personas are paradoxical because they need the exact opposite conditions to be nourished. The explorer must move and the homebody must stay still. This contradiction causes tension in our mental landscape because it is impossible to please both simultaneously. When we are travelling we long to be home and when we are home we long to travel. And yet in a strange way these two are bound to each other and share the same territory. Without an explorer as a partner for our

If we are travelling through a space that has been highly rationalized, the 'story' is mono-dimensional, flat, and over-familiar.

The streets became an outward expression of internal contradictions, a marginal territory that was the mirror image of internal marginal territory.

homebody, our home would become a prison, and without a homebody as a partner for our explorer, our explorer would become a vagabond in permanent exile. The mental space in which these two personas dance with each other is marginal territory, a borderland.

In traditional city building, the contradictory needs of traveller and homebody were allowed to share the same street space with no attempt to rationalize them. The streets became an outward expression of the internal contradictions, a marginal territory that was the mirror image of internal marginal territory. In fact, the streets became a space in which citizens could creatively resolve their internal contradiction between explorer and homebody. The public spaces they moved through became part of their home territory. While moving through other people's home territory, they partook of the sense of home created by the residents. At the same time, as traveller they enriched the experience of those whose home territory they passed through by bringing movement, colour, goods, friendship, and stories. Instead of an ever-shrinking home territory, this arrangement allowed for an ever-expanding sense of home while at the same time satisfying some of the needs of the explorer. This was particularly true for children. As they matured they were given increasing licence to explore their neighbourhood and beyond. These 'regions beyond' were then integrated into the mental map of their home territory. So both these contradictory needs were met simultaneously – the need for adventure and the need for home.

The most interesting and engaging public spaces are those that connect us to the most fundamental paradoxes in our minds: the clash between our need for order and our need for spontaneity; our need to move and our need to stay still; our need for solitude and our need for intimacy; our need to be known and our need to be anonymous; our need for the sacred and our need for the profane; our need for reason and our need for absurdity. When public space creates a borderland in which these contradictory needs share the same space, it connects us to the rhythm of life itself, a rhythm that moves to a very slow beat. In these spaces we are forced to pause and dance with the impossible for a moment.

And the greater the number of paradoxical roles built into the space, the richer and denser it becomes. The borderlands are always pregnant with possibilities.

The most interesting and engaging public spaces are those that connect us to the most fundamental paradoxes in our minds.

It is fundamentally unhealthy to rationalize our identity and purge ourselves of contradictions.

Creating borderlands in people's minds

In the last chapter I argued that traffic is first and foremost a social and cultural problem. Here I come to the very core of the issue. Just as our culture has tried to rationalize space and eliminate the borderlands in our urban environments, it has tried to do the same with the spaces in our mind. We try to eliminate our internal contradictions. People who are considered to have their act together are people who have established a strong identity for themselves, an identity that has been purged of internal contradictions. Through reason they have sorted out what they really want in life. If people can't make up their minds what they want, we say, `For goodness sake sort yourself out and make up your mind what you really want'.

I believe that it is fundamentally unhealthy to rationalize our identity and purge ourselves of contradictions – just as it is fundamentally unhealthy for the built environment. Our need to move and our need to reside are both legitimate human needs rooted deep in our psyche. So is our need for intimacy and our need for solitude; or our need for order and our need for spontaneity. In rationalizing these paradoxes, we are forced to submerge a legitimate need and lock it up in the basement. We also destroy the borderlands in our mind, the tidal mudflats of our creativity.

As a culture, we have developed some strange ways of rationalizing our internal contradictions. One is to play the Jekyll-and-Hyde game where we flip-flop between our contradictory personas. When Jeckyll is dominant, Hyde is locked firmly in the basement, where he plots the overthrow of Jeckyll. Hyde breaks out and immediately assigns Jekyll to

the basement. The Jekyll-and-Hyde game is only successful if the two personas have their own very clearly defined
mental and physical spaces and are not allowed to stray
into each other's space – one of the major reasons we have
created very distinct spaces for moving and very distinct
spaces for residing.

In western culture it appears like the explorer or traveller is the dominant voice – the one in control most of the
time. The homebody appears to be subordinate. However,
Jung argued that what we suppress in the basement will
always find a way to exert its will covertly, but that this
will be in a subversive and destructive way. So has the
homebody found a covert way of exerting its dominance
even while been locked in the basement? It appears so.
Masquerading as an explorer and traveller, the homebody
uses the car to take their home with them into the public domain. But by
entering public space in a privacy bubble, the homebody, masquerading
as an explorer, reduces the potential for spontaneous life and discovery in
that space. In an ironic twist they sabotage their own desires by degrading
the public realm as both a place to explore and as a place to reside. Instead
of public space providing an ever-expanding sense of home, homebodies
shrink their own home territory. The homebody reacts by fortifying what
little home territory they have left, further reducing the vibrancy of the
public realm and further shrinking their sense of home.

In my opinion, one of the major causes of traffic problems in neighbourhoods is that cities are aiding and abetting their citizens in playing

One of the major causes of traffic problems in neighbourhoods is that cities are aiding and abetting their citizens in playing the Jekyll–and–Hyde game.

the Jekyll–and-Hyde game in at least three important ways.

1. When residents come to the city (in their homebody persona) and complain about traffic, the city says: 'Oh yes, we will fix those bad motorists for you. We will traffic calm your street'. The city does not ask the residents to internalize the conflict between homebody and motorist. Instead the city helps the residents treat this problem as an external conflict between themselves as residents and another group of residents that happen to be in their motoring persona.

2. In consultation processes, and in the political process, the city treats people as if they had a single unified identity with a single unified set of values and needs. In many cases, the steering group for a study will have people representing 'residents' and other people representing 'motorists'; some people will represent the 'environmentalists' and other people will represent 'business people'. An adversarial relationship is set up between these people and the process becomes a war to see which side 'wins'. New forms of consultation would internalize this conflict that has become externalized. If internalized, the energy generated by the conflict between our contradictory desires would not be wasted in a battle of egos, but would be harnessed to generate innovations to deal more creatively with the tension.

3. In creating mono-functional spaces (spaces that are clearly defined as living space or movement space) the city facilitates people being able to more easily slip from their resident persona into their motoring persona, and vice versa, without the two needing to share the same space. If the two were forced to share the same space they may be forced to form a more civil relationship.

The first step in tackling traffic problems is to internalize what has become an external conflict, and this means deliberately creating borderlands in both the physical realm and in people's minds. This is not necessarily a rational process. Here is just one example of how this can be done.

Together with a group of residents in Boise, Idaho, I co-invented the Neighbourhood Pace Car. This was an evolutionary adaptation of the Neighbourhood Treaty that we tried in Henry Street. Residents sign a pledge to drive within the speed limit, be courteous to other road users and reduce their car use to a minimum. They get a Pace Car sticker to put on the back of their car to let those behind know why they are driving courteously. We explain to the residents that their car becomes a 'mobile speed bump' – an intelligent one that gets out of the way of emergency vehicles. When enough people sign the Pace Car Pledge, traffic will be calmed citywide. Now when I offer this program to a group of residents who have a traffic problem on their street, you see their chest puff out. Their immediate response is: 'Give me one of those stickers. I want to be in charge of how fast the traffic goes on my street'. This is their 'resident' or 'homebody' persona responding because the Pace Car program gives this submerged voice power. About ten seconds later you see something happening behind their eyes. The 'motoring' persona in their head suddenly puts two and two together. 'Like hell you are putting one of those stickers on the car. That means you have to drive everywhere within

Without them even knowing it, we have created a space in their mind, a borderland, where their resident and motoring persona are forced into a dialogue about their competing needs and desires.

the speed limit!'. The debate rages inside their head, sometimes for weeks or even months. Whether they eventually sign the pledge or not is almost immaterial. Without them even knowing it, we have created a space in their mind, a borderland, where their resident and motoring persona are forced into a dialogue about their competing needs and desires. The Pace Car program creates a space in which these two voices can dialogue in a civil manner.

Note that creating this borderland space in the mental domain is not a rational process. In fact it can't be because there is never a logical way to embrace contradictory desires. We do not go to people and say, 'Do you realize you have a split personality? You have a motorist in your head that loves speed and a resident in your head that hates speed. Now let's get these two together and have a rational conversation about how both their needs can be met'. Instead we legitimize the submerged voice and give it space in which to dialogue with the dominant voice as an equal. What was an external conflict has now been internalized.

One of the greatest challenges facing cities is how to translate this understanding into the way authorities conduct community consultation. Current political structures are built around adversarial relationships in which people adopt a single unified identity. This book is not the place to explore further what I call creating the Third Space (the borderlands), but essentially it is about creating processes and physical spaces that allow for people's contradictory needs to enter a meaningful dialogue. When my friends tell me they want X, I ask them if there is another part of them that wants the exact opposite. This allows us to explore the complex landscape of their desires. We need political processes that allow us to do this as a total community. We not only need to create the borderlands in people's minds, and in physical space. We also need to create the borderlands in the political life of the community.

In my opinion, the most interesting people are those who have embraced their internal contradictions. In fact, the greater the contradictions the more interesting and engaging the person becomes. The best public spaces work the same. They welcome both the child and the wise elder; the traveller and the resident; the jester and the mystic; the storyteller and the voice of reason. They contain both order and chaos; legibility and ambiguity. They are the mirror image of our own borderlands, the tidal mudflats where new life can emerge.

For sometime after meeting Hans Monderman, I puzzled over the parallels in our lives, particularly our marginal experiences as children and our choice to continue living in the borderlands. I wondered why both of us had come up with a radical new approach to the design of our streets. And then I came up with a hypothesis.

Perhaps Hans and I represent a prominent aspect of our culture – we have become the mobile generation. However, our yearning and need for a sense of home becomes more pressing the more mobile we become. And maybe, because both of us are prepared to embrace the borderlands, we have allowed these contradictory worlds to collide in our minds – and in the streets we design. These streets are not rationalized, linear spaces that are for either moving along or residing in. Instead they become the borderlands in which our internal contradictions find a home.

Three Maps

Following my day with Hans, I visited a number of Dutch cities where I observed something that struck me as being very strange. Dutch houses, town houses and apartments are much closer to the sidewalk than they are in Australia. And each one had an oversized front window (oversized from my perspective). But what was striking was that most of these windows did not have curtains. Walking down the sidewalk you could look straight into people's living areas and see half-finished meals on the table, or toys strewn all over the floor, or, in one case, I could read the titles of the person's favourite books. Furthermore, many of these windows contained some kind of display that was not faced into the room, but faced outward to the street; displays such as collections of antiques, dolls, or plants. These displays revealed something about the personality of the people who lived in that house and they were a gift to the community.

This blurring of the boundary between private and public space was particularly striking for me because in Australia we tend to fence our private space off and in new housing developments, the only thing that addresses the street directly is the double or triple garage doors which are open and shut with a remote control.

In Delft I walked past one house and saw a half-finished sculpture of a pregnant lady in a window. I was tempted to take a photo because it epitomized so well the whole concept of borderlands and blurring the boundaries. But there were three people talking on the sidewalk, just next door, and I felt uncomfortable with the thought of standing there at the naked window taking pictures of the inside of the house. So I walked on. Then I said to myself: 'That was too good a picture to miss. Go back and ask the three people talking if they think the owner would mind you taking a picture'.

I walked back up the street, but before I could even ask, one of the three said, 'Can I help you'?

I replied, 'I study urban design and I would love a picture of that sculpture in the window. Do you think the owner would mind'?

'Oh, you can't do that', one of them replied emphatically. 'That is her private art. You would need to ask her but she left just a couple minutes ago'.

At first I thought this response was strange. Why would the artist put her private art on public display? But then it made sense. What allowed these Dutch citizens to blur the boundaries between private and public was a strong sense of boundary at the social level. While the physical boundaries were blurred, at the social level it was very clear what liberties one could take in this ambiguous zone. You can peek in, but you would not stand there and stare.

I tell this story, not to continue my discussion on borderlands, but to introduce another concept. Why do the Dutch build their houses very differently to the way we build them in Australia? Why do they address the street with a display window and we address the street with a blank wall and remote-controlled garage doors? Why do the Dutch build bikeways and multi-storey bike parking stations while Americans build bigger freeways and multi-storey car parking stations?

In workshops I conduct with planning professionals, I answer this crucial question by getting participants to pretend that they are a group of anthropologists examining the African tribal compound of the Ambo people (see below). I ask them to see what they can tell about the beliefs, culture and mythologies of the Ambo people just by looking at this diagram. Try it yourself before reading on.

There is a lot you can tell about the Ambo people by looking at the physical layout of their kraal. They put a high value on cattle. They are polygamous. Conversation and social interaction are central to the life of

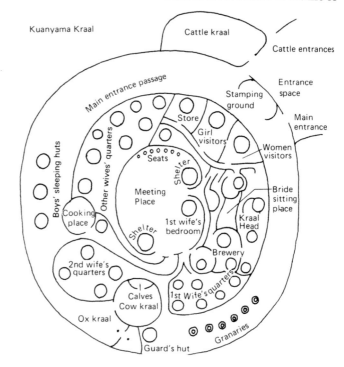

Chiefly kraal of the Ambo people. Source: The Social Logic of Space. *Hillier & Hanson. Cambridge University Press, 1984. Page 164.*

the kraal. Alcohol is a highly valued commodity (the brewery is closer to the kraal head's sleeping quarters than the first wife's sleeping quarters). Everything we build, from our individual house to large cities, contains a 'body language' that tells us about our 'mental topography' – our beliefs, values, mythologies, and thinking paradigms. Societies can only exist as they take on a physical and material form in the spatial realm. A built environment is not just an artefact of a society. It is the 'body' of that society which facilitates both internal and external relationships. There is, therefore, a symbiotic relationship between three landscapes: the built landscape, the mental landscape and the social landscape.

There is a symbiotic relationship between three landscapes: the built landscape, the mental landscape and the social landscape.

To understand the symbiotic relationship between these three domains, let's explore an example that I have already given in this book. I have said that part of our mental landscape (both as individuals and as a society) is that we believe healthy people have a single unified identity. We therefore put labels on ourselves and others: 'I am a resident and he is a motorist'.

This belief system – part of our mental map – is then built into our physical environment: 'This is my space as a resident and that is your space as a motorist'. These spaces need to be clearly defined because they are kept separate in our mental landscape.

Our beliefs, and the physical environments that this dictates, then shape social reality: 'I am a resident and you are a motorist, and I hate what your traffic is doing to my quality of life as a resident. I am going to put pressure on my city to forcibly calm you'. Because the city sees this as a conflict between two groups of people (each with a single unified identity) it creates an adversarial political and consultation process that reinforces

The most efficient and effective way of addressing problems in the spatial realm is almost always to address their source in the mental and social domain.

and reflects our mental and spatial landscapes. To even participate in the political/social process we must first decide if we are going to the public meeting or public hearing as a 'resident' or 'motorist'.

I said that these three maps are symbiotic. This means that there is a dynamic relationship between all three. In the example I am giving, the externalizing of conflict between the resident and motorist has resulted in changes to our streets (spatial map). We install traffic calming devices such as speed bumps to forcibly calm the motorists. The social conflict has incarnated into our physical environment. This change to the physical environment then reinforces our mental map of the conflict between resident and motorist as being an external conflict.

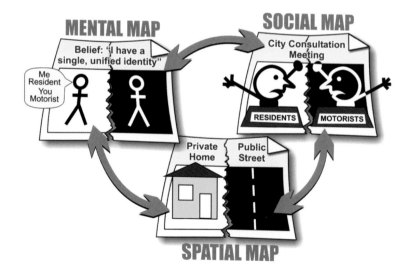

In the past, design professionals felt that a problem in the spatial realm (for example, traffic congestion around a school) was best dealt with by making changes to the physical design of the space (build a drop off zone, or create safe routes to school). But what the three maps discovery tells us, and what I have argued already in this book, is that problems in the spatial realm usually have their genesis in the mental and social realm. For example, the traffic jams around the school are being driven largely by parents' perceptions about road danger and stranger danger. These perceptions are part of the mental maps of these parents. They are also an expression of the social maps – the perceptions are created, to some degree, by the way events are reported in the media. It was this insight that led me to invent the Walking School Bus, a social arrangement that addresses perceptions by creating a piece of social infrastructure. I have shown how the speed of traffic on streets is largely governed by the degree of psychological retreat of the residents. Again this is part of the mental map of these residents. It is doubtful whether speed bumps would reverse this psychological retreat. But a street party often does – an event in the social realm. In fact I believe that the most efficient and effective way of addressing problems in the spatial realm is almost always to address their source in the mental and social domain.

Some people may be left wondering if there is a place for design and working in the physical domain. Absolutely, but with qualifications. As I have shown, design of the physical realm can create a borderland in which our internal contradictions are given a voice. However, the more suppressed a particular voice has become in the social and mental landscapes, the greater the need to overtly tie the design to a social program. For example, when Hans Monderman asked the design professionals to make the main street of Oudehaske 'more like a traditional village street' he was asking them to give physical expression to a very long and strong tradition in Holland of seeing streets as an extension of people's living room. This tradition is preserved in the way people treat their front display window. Now Hans has a very strong social program as part of his design process – a fact that is overlooked by most people who go to see the streets he designs. But in Australia or North America we are dealing with a very different mental topography than Hans – one in which the resident voice has become much more submerged than it is in Holland. This means that we need an even stronger social program to lead the design process. This social program will work first and foremost with people's mental maps. It will deal with our submerged desires and the inappropriate ways we have tried to satisfy those desires.

Rooms and Corridors

After my time in Holland with Hans, I traveled through a number of European cities before arriving in Munich. To modern planners, the streets of these cities seem chaotic and 'unplanned'. As I stood looking at the cathedrals and other magnificent public buildings in Munich, I thought how strange it was to think that these people were capable of designing and constructing magnificent cathedrals, but when it comes to street design they were totally incompetent. The truth is they were using a different mental map when designing their streets than the map we may use. For them, streets were not just for going places, they were places. They were not just for movement, they were also for residing. This mental map produced a very different street design that has it own internal logic.

This mental map produced a very different street design that has it own internal logic.

Earlier I discussed how cities are 'an invention to maximize exchanges and minimize travel'. Cities have two types of space; exchange space and movement space. The more of a city handed over to movement space the less efficient it becomes as a mechanism for facilitating exchanges. Early city builders used the same technique that architects use to minimize movement space in a building; they broke down the walls that divided a space and created dual purpose space – space which can be used for

both movement and exchange. This development produced a new kind of exchange that greatly enhanced the efficiency of the city – the spontaneous exchange.

Now if you are creating a room in your house that performs the dual function of movement and exchange, do you make it look like a room or a corridor? Because the central function of any room in a house is to facilitate exchanges, and the subservient function is movement, the room is designed primarily around facilitating exchanges. Exactly the same logic was used in creating streets in older cities. Whether it is in Venice, Munich, Florence, Paris or a small Dutch village, as you walk down a street you have the feeling of passing through a series of interconnected rooms. You go through some kind of a narrowed entryway and enter a 'room'. In the 'walls' of this room, you will see 'doorways' that lead you to other 'rooms'. The streets of these older cities only seem chaotic to us because we are using a different mental map: we think of streets as 'corridors' and corridors need to be much more logical and linear. Streets that act as outdoor living rooms need to feel enclosed and intimate. They need to have their own unique character and be full of spontaneous surprises. Ironically, the only way for early city builders to build such streets was to allow them to grow organically and spontaneously rather than rationalizing them and 'planning' them.

Where did this change from seeing streets as room to seeing them as corridors come from? We can hypothesize that it came in part from the Industrial Revolution, when the city began to be viewed more as a machine for the production of consumer goods and less as a place where great civilizations were born and nurtured. 'Efficiency' was measured in

The streets of these older cities only seem chaotic to us because we are using a different mental map.

narrow, isolated terms, rather than seeing the efficiency of the entire system. Value was placed on 'movement' because it carried with it connotations of 'progress'. To be resident was to stand still and to stand still was to stagnate.

Since our mental maps give shape, unconsciously, to our physical landscape, we have created streets that look, feel and act as corridors rather than looking, feeling and acting like rooms. Any change in our mental maps about our streets is going to demand a radically new design approach to our streets, one that turns the corridors into rooms.

The Safety Paradox

My arguments about deliberately using intrigue and uncertainty as mental speed bumps to slow motorists fly in the face of current perceived wisdom about safety – to make streets safer they need to be made more predictable. The reaction I get from planning professionals and even lay people, is totally predictable: 'But doesn't creating intrigue and uncertainty cause accidents? When there is an accident on a freeway, people rubberneck and this causes yet another accident'.

One of the interesting things about the work that I do is that questions like this are my greatest teacher. Often I find that they contain an element of truth, which forces me to build a more complex and more robust 'mental map' and this is exactly what happened with the rubbernecking question. I discovered that when it comes to safety, there is a paradox. In some situations, you can make environments safer by making them more predictable. But in other environments, making them more predictable makes them less safe. How can making one environment more predictable make it safer but make another less safe?

The key to unraveling the safety paradox is to understand the concept of 'false sense of security'. False sense of security is when something appears safer than it is in reality and we are tricked into taking a risk that

The key to unraveling the safety paradox is to understand the concept of 'false sense of security'.

What made the event unsafe was not that kids were playing with balls in a street.

we would not have taken if we had known the true state of affairs. As a kid, you probably stood on a branch while climbing a tree that looked strong enough to hold you. But inside it was rotten, and the branch broke. The branch lulled you into a false sense of security because the branch looked stronger than it really was. Similarly, when we put the 274 traffic cones up the centre of the street in Boise, Idaho, we created a false sense of security by making the environment look more predictable and safer than it was in reality. The cones created a false impression because just a few metres from the speeding traffic were children playing with bikes and balls. What made the event unsafe was not that kids were playing with balls in a street. We had done that many times before in complete safety. The event was made so unsafe by the false messages about predictability conveyed by the cones and signs.

The design of any space conveys a subconscious message to those using the space about the 'normative state' of that environment – what can be reasonably expected. When we are on a freeway, the design makes a covert promise that we can expect high levels of predictability. Pedestrians, cyclists and farm machinery have been banned. High noise barriers shield us from the distractions of normal neighbourhood life. The design rationale for these kind of roads has been to remove all unpredictability and make them as predictable as possible. Through the design we are making a covert promise to motorists: 'This is a predictable environment in which you are highly unlikely to encounter the unpredictable'. The motorists, therefore, drive according to these perceptions. On a whole, removing the unpredictable from this environment does make it safer. However, if the motorists are suddenly confronted with the unpredictable or an element of intrigue (such as an accident, or a stray animal), they are in the wrong mental state to deal with this. Their senses are not on high alert and they are travelling too fast to deal with this unexpected distraction. Intrigue in this setting does cause rubbernecking which does cause accidents.

But the situation is reversed in a neighbourhood street – or what Hans refers to as the social world. If a motorist is driving down a residential street and sees children's toys on the side of the street, or kids playing in the street, the visual clues send a covert message that: 'this is a space in which the unexpected should be expected'. The motorist immediately slows down to accommodate the possibility of the unexpected happening.

So the key to solving the seeming contradiction in the safety paradox is to understand that safety is maximized when false sense of security is minimized. And in the traffic world, false sense of security is minimized

Safety is maximized when false sense of security is minimized.

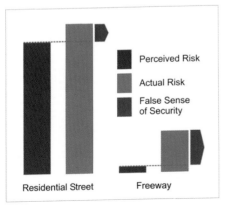

Perceived Risk

Actual Risk

False Sense of Security

Residential Street   Freeway

False sense of security is the difference between actual risk and perceived risk. False sense of security is not dependent on the actual amount of risk in the environment. Hypothetically, a freeway could have a greater false sense of security than a residential street. Or vice versa.

Line markings, official signage, concrete islands and even first-generation traffic calming devices create a mixed message.

by removing unpredictable events (make reality more closely fit the perceptions). But in the social world, false sense of security is minimized by removing elements that make a false promise of predictability to the motorists (make the perceptions more closely match the reality). In the neighbourhood setting, there are three basic ways in which perceptions about the degree of uncertainty can be signalled.

— Permanent overt indicators: sidewalks, trees, and design elements that signal 'room' rather than 'corridor' (entryway, ceiling, strong walls, floor design, furniture, art, and the telltale signs of everyday life).

— Permanent covert indicators: lack of signs, regulations and traffic control devices. Streetscapes that are ever-changing – art and furniture is changed regularly.

— Temporary indicators: human activity, movable street reclaiming art and furniture.

In establishing clear signals about the normative state of a street, what is not included is often more important that what is. If the normative state is that the unexpected should be expected, then traffic control devices such as line markings, official signage, concrete islands and even first-generation traffic calming devices create a mixed message. They covertly promise motorists a certain levels of predictability. Ambiguity and lack of clear direction can be incredibly important visual clues as to the 'normative state' of a space.

Why not make neighbourhood streets more predictable

So far I have skirted a very important question: why shouldn't we use the same strategy we use to make freeways safer on neighbourhood streets

– that is, make them more predictable in reality by controlling the amount of intrigue and uncertainty that the motorist is exposed too?

Social life, by its very nature, is composed of two types of exchanges, what I have termed the planned exchange and the spontaneous exchange. Much of a city's life resolves around planned exchanges: meetings, work, some shopping, and maybe a dinner party. But as writers such as Jane Jacobs have shown, almost all neighbourhood life revolves around the spontaneous or unplanned exchange. In fact, the quality of neighbourhood life can be measured by the health of the spontaneous exchange realm. Sure there are some planned exchanges in neighbourhoods, like a public meeting or a street party. But even these planned events are heavily interlaced with spontaneous exchanges.

The quality of neighbourhood life can be measured by the health of the spontaneous exchange realm.

Jane Jacobs, in her landmark book *The Death and Life of Great American Cities*, tells how people in New York will leave their house keys with the butcher, or the newsagent, or the hairdresser. Many of these store owners even have a special drawer in which they keep people's house keys. Jane Jacobs asks where this trust comes from. She argues that this trust is built out of random encounters in the street, much of it trivial. But the sum of these spontaneous encounters is not trivial. It creates a feeling of public identity and a 'web of public respect and trust' which becomes 'a resource in time of personal or neighbourhood need'.

Because unless we also make the social life of the street more controlled and predictable we will simply create a false sense of security.

In the book *Street Reclaiming* I showed how the spontaneous exchange realm of neighbourhoods is fundamental to the personal development of children, the democratic process, social equity, and the ability of the elderly to share their wisdom with others. By very definition, spontaneous exchanges have high levels of intrigue and uncertainty. So let me answer the question about why it is inappropriate to try to make neighbourhood streets safer by making them more predictable. Because unless we also make the social life of the street more controlled and predictable we will simply create a false sense of security. Authorities cannot have it both ways. If they seriously believe that intrigue and uncertainty cause accidents, then we must ban people from using the sidewalk and every house should be fenced in a way that does not allow drivers to be distracted by activity in the front yard. In fact, all houses should be painted a uniform colour to reduce distraction. And the Dutch should certainly be forced to put curtains on their windows!

If you desire vibrant neighbourhoods and safe streets there is only one road ahead: intrigue, uncertainty, humour and lots of blurred boundaries.

Design of a street can be a self-fulfilling prophecy. Traffic oriented devices send motorists a covert message – this space is predictable and primarily for traffic. Speeds automatically rise. Community life will retreat from this space, which further increases predictability, which further increases speed. On the other hand, create a street environment with high levels of ambiguity and traffic speeds will drop and community life will blossom in this space. So the amount of intrigue and uncertainty signalled by the design of a traffic environment must be determined by

The same officials are not removing traffic control devices across the city because they engender a false sense of security in the motorist!

the vision of the vibrancy of community and economic life desired for a space, not by current levels of intrigue and uncertainty. The current levels may well be the result of previous design decisions.

Let me address a very important issue about false sense of security, one that helps us understand the dynamics a little better. Many city officials have begun reducing the number of pedestrian crossings on the basis that they engender a false sense of security in the pedestrian, which leads to higher accident rates. While this is true to some extent, the same officials are not removing traffic control devices across the city because they engender a false sense of security in the motorist! The pedestrian crossing debate has been a classic case of blame the victim. No accident at a pedestrian crossing, where the pedestrian is obeying the law, should be blamed on the pedestrian, regardless of whether they are feeling a 'false sense of security' or not. It is the motorist who is not taking due care, and this is partly because the motorist has already been lulled into a false sense of security before they get to the pedestrian crossing. The motorist's false sense of security has been engendered by two inter-related facts: there are not enough design signals that pedestrians are present, and all the design signals tell the motorist that this is their space and that they are in a predictable environment. Simply removing the pedestrian crossing and forcing the pedestrian to increase their level of vigilance while doing nothing to increase the vigilance of the driver is a grossly unjust way to tackle pedestrian crossing deaths. In fact, the current policy of removing crossings is totally counterproductive when you consider the big picture. It actually promises the driver greater levels of predictability by removing any visual clues about the presence of pedestrians (which are already too scant). While removing the crossing diminishes the pedestrian's false sense of security it increases the drivers false sense of security even further.

Having said this, I am not advocating more pedestrian crossings. Quite the contrary. I have argued that the entire street design should make it clear that the space is primarily a people space and that motorists should act as guests in this space. The pedestrian crossing, to some extent, helps reinforce the message that the space is primarily for traffic and that people space is tightly controlled and regulated. However, if an authority is not willing to make this larger change, the pedestrian crossing is a lesser of two evils.

About risk

Introducing more intrigue and uncertainty into a street does not mean that motorists will adjust their speed to a level that eliminates all risk. (The same people who take unacceptable risks on the freeway will take unacceptable risks in a residential street full of children.) The truth is that we all add a certain 'risk factor' to what we perceive to be 'safe'. Make our vehicle or travel environment 'safer' and we will travel faster (we add the same amount of risk to the new safety level). But the opposite is also true. Make our travel environment feel less predictable and we will travel slower. We will still be taking the same amount of risk as before, but we will be going slower. Because we are adding the same amount of risk factor as before, we will have

Make our travel environment feel less predictable and we will travel slower.

(on average) about the same number of accidents. However, because the speed is slower the accidents are likely to be less severe.

Towards a Safety Hypothesis

There are a number of factors that determine the overall risk of death or injury that people expose themselves to when driving.

— **FSS Factor** (False Sense of Security).

— **PN Factor** (The Propensity to take risk multiplied by the Need to take risk). We all have a different propensity to take risk depending on our temperament, mood and social/cultural setting. Our need to take risk is determined by our immediate life circumstances (for example, the amount of risk we are prepared to take will be different if our child is bleeding to death, than if we are running late for a casual lunch with a friend). The amount of risk we take at any moment in time is a combination of propensity and need.

— **IR Factor** (Imposed Risk). This is the risk imposed by others for which we cannot compensate.

— **Speed Factor.** While this is determined to some extent by the above factors, it is also determined by the design of the driving environment and the design of the vehicle.

The total danger that a particular person is exposed to is a combination of all the above factors. My hypothesis of how these factors relate to each other is this:

Total Danger = ((FSS x PN) + IR) x Speed

This means that in terms of safety, an authority can take specific steps to reduce each of these risk factors.

— Reduce False Sense of Security by having the design signal to the driver that they are likely to encounter high levels of unpredictability. The greater the level of unpredictability likely to be encountered, the greater the ambiguity required in the design.

— Promote such high levels of human activity that the intrigue and uncertainty generated by the activity overpower contrary design signals.

— Reduce the propensity for people to take risks through education and social programs. Behaviour modification programs such as the Pace Car program can reduce people's propensity to add risk.

— Add new risk factors and increase perceptions of these 'risks'. This may be the risk of social censure – my peers will think I am antisocial if I drive fast.

— Teach people how to mitigate or compensate for the risk imposed by others (eg Defensive Driving Courses or cycling classes for students).

— Bring speeds down by introducing new elements of intrigue and uncertainty and/or by reducing the design speed of the environment and vehicle.

Beyond Fundamentalism
– the Design Paradox

Some years ago I ran a series of workshops for planning professionals. One of the exercises in this workshop was to divide the audience into small groups. Half the people in these small groups would retain their existing identity as planners. The other half would pretend they were aliens from a planet where there was no such thing as a planning profession. The aliens would cross-examine the planners to find out what it is on planet earth that led to the emergence of 'planners'.

After much discussion between the aliens and planners, at least one group of aliens would report back: 'We have concluded that planning is some kind of religion and that the planners are the high priests of this religion. Their bible is the Highway Design Manual. It contains rules that have been handed down from on high. No one knows where these rules came from but they are obviously divinely inspired'.

Everyone would laugh. I would then sketch the history of city planning. In the first cities, the priest-astrologer and city planner was one and the same profession. The great public works programs of all ancient civilizations were driven by a priesthood who discerned cosmic order

'We have concluded that planning is some kind of religion and that the planners are the high priests of this religion'.

Fundamentalist planning, like fundamentalist religion, is built on dogma and the need for certainty.

then used sacred geometry to communicate this cosmic order. The modern town planning movement, which emerged at the beginning of the twentieth century, was driven by social reformers with strong religious beliefs. The theological background of each of these social reformers shaped their vision of the Utopian city.

Urban planning has retained one element of its religious roots – fundamentalism. Planning fashions have come and gone. But regardless of the fashion, it has been driven by design dogmas that are often embraced with fundamentalist zeal. Having spent 38 years of my life entrenched in religious fundamentalism, I have an intimate knowledge of fundamentalism. Fundamentalism is a grasp for certainty. It reduces the rich complexity of life to a small number of 'fundamental truths'. Instead of wrestling with the unfathomable paradoxes inherent in all of life, it creates a simple world of black and white, right and wrong, either or. Fundamentalist planning, like fundamentalist religion, is built on dogma and the need for certainty.

Marked bike lanes make it safer for cyclists.

Sidewalks make it safer for pedestrians.

Pedestrian crossings make it safer for pedestrians.

Let me take bike lanes as a way of illustrating how the 'real world' is very different from the simplistic world of fundamentalist planning. At first glance it seems self-evident that bike lanes automatically make streets safer for cyclists. It is common knowledge that the wider the traffic lane, the faster a motorist will tend to go. Narrowing traffic lanes by painting bike lanes increases what engineers call 'friction'. The narrower a passage way the slower we tend to go because there is not the same margin for error. Note that narrowing a lane to bring speeds down relies on a mental response from the motorist to the *perception* that danger has increased.

But there is a contradictory psychological impact of bike lanes. They deliver greater certainty to the driver. The driver knows exactly which is cyclists' space and which is their space. This increased certainty about where the cyclist will be in the roadway encourages the motorist to speed up.

So narrowing the lane width tells the motorist to slow down, but the increased certainty about where the cyclist will be tells them to speed up. Some studies show that the net result of these contradictory psychological factors is that, depending on the original design of the street, speeds may go up, down, or stay the same.

The new approach to design is fascinated by how complex and contradictory psychological factors play themselves out in the heads of those using a public space.

But there is another interesting set of contradictory factors when it comes to bike lanes. Bike lanes change the perceptions of the cyclist. Cyclists feel safer because they no longer have to share a space with motorists. But as a Swedish study found, this is to some extent a false sense of security. The study found that when bike lanes are present, motorists impose greater risks on the cyclists, for example, driving closer to the cyclist when passing. Does this then mean that accident rates go up after the bike lane goes in? Not necessarily. Because the cyclists feel safer, more of them cycle on that street. A British study found that as cycling rates go up, accident rates per trip plummet because you raise the motorists' expectation that there may be a cyclist just around the corner, even when there is not a cyclist in sight.

So bike lanes seduce motorists into transferring risk onto the cyclists. But the increased numbers of cyclists seduces the motorists into taking more care.

So you can see from this cursory exploration of bike lanes that there is at least four paradoxical factors at work – and maybe many more than this. Understanding this complexity has caused me to declare myself a 'bike lane agnostic'. Whether the negatives outweigh the positives, or vice versa, is completely dependent on the context – traffic volumes, bike volumes, current design of the street, and the social and cultural context. Including or not including bike lanes requires creating a total design package that does not just focus on design of the physical environment, but includes dealing with the mental maps and social maps of cyclists,

Some of the most lively public spaces in the world break the 'rules' for good design. In the great Sienna square, you must sit on the ground. And in Portland (far right), the city that pioneered regulations banning blank walls because they kill street life, you can find this dynamic coffee shop.

motorists and residents. For example, the fact that cyclists feel safer may be an important consideration.

Exactly the same paradoxes apply to pedestrian crossings and even sidewalks. On all these design issues I give myself permission to be an agnostic.

I recently visited a small city in Canada where the local bike organization had fought for several years to get bike lanes on King Street, a road that was been widened through their city. They felt like they had suffered a huge defeat when the Province did not include bike lanes. I explained that they could actually use the lack of bike lanes to make the road safer for cyclists. How on earth can you use lack of cycle lanes to make a street safer? You start by identifying the safety pluses and safety

Understanding this complexity has caused me to declare myself a 'bike lane agnostic'.

minuses of bike lanes then find other ways to deliver the safety benefits while avoiding the safety minuses.

The first safety plus of bike lanes is that the presence of the lane and the bike symbols stencilled in the lane are a constant reminder to motorists that their might be cyclists around. This increases the motorist's expectation and vigilance. The group decided that they could achieve this safety benefit by adopting King Street (in North America groups adopt sections of highway and remove litter) then placing bike sculptures along the length of the roadway.

The second safety plus of bike lanes is that cyclists perceive that the bike lane makes it safer. More people cycle, which increases the motorist's expectation levels and vigilance. The group decided they could achieve this same safety plus by having an 'Eccentric Cyclists on King Street' event every Monday. Members of their organization would be encouraged to dress eccentrically or do something humorous to their bicycle, and even if it meant going slightly out of their way, deliberately ride on King Street on Mondays. They would approach the local radio station to see if they would sponsor a competition for drivers to ring in and report sightings of eccentric cyclists on King Street. This would give cyclists a feeling of safety in numbers, meaning more cyclists would cycle. The eccentric dress and radio competition would raise the expectation in motorist's minds that there may be a cyclist just around the corner.

You will notice that both these initiatives are social initiatives, even though the sculptures involved physical design. It is my personal opinion that if implemented, these two social programs would deliver greater safety benefits than painted bike lanes could ever have delivered because it maximizes the safety pluses of bike lanes and minimizes the safety negatives.

One of the very impressive elements of the new approach to design practiced by Hans Monderman and his colleagues in Europe is a distinct move away from planning fundamentalism. I recently visited a number of cities and villages experimenting with what is now being called Shared Space. Generally speaking, bollards are not used in this new design approach because they create too strong a distinction between pedestrian space and drivers space. But in Haren I saw small sections of 'fencing' dividing the sidewalk from the road. It was explained that they were needed to stop motorists parking on the sidewalk. And they were deliberately designed to serve a secondary function – bike racks. In order to

A Hans Monderman design showing how each design is very site specific. Here the street is made an integral part of the park on the left. Hans is fond of saying that the street must 'tell the story' of its surroundings. Because each location is unique, there can be no standardized designs.

It is comfortable in the borderlands where certainty is replaced with dynamic life.

compensate for this perceived barrier between the two spaces, the curb was done away with entirely, making the sidewalk and road flow into each other at exactly the same level.

This design in Haren also included a number of painted pedestrian crossings. Hans explained that while he was against such traffic devices, in this case there were a number of elderly people who felt like they needed this extra security. So the city engineer created the crossings using a paint that will wear off in time, hoping that by the time it wears off, the elderly residents will feel more confident. This illustrates how mental speed bumps or shared space is emerging as an exciting cross-disciplinary field. It treats the connection between people's mental maps, social maps and spatial maps as interdependent and totally dynamic. It avoids the mistake of one design of physical space fits all. It embraces the contradictions in all three landscapes as a drive to greater creativity. It is comfortable in the borderlands where certainty is replaced with dynamic life.

So You Don't Live in a Dutch Village

On my first trip with Hans, he said that he was not sure how his design approach would translate into other cities. We are now ready to tackle this key issue. There are four key differences between the Dutch villages in which Hans is working and a typical North American, Australian, UK, New Zealand, or any modern city. Dealing with these differences gives us some clues as to how we may go about creating mental speed bumps and taming traffic in these contexts. I have already laid the foundations for understanding these differences.

Before examining these differences I should sound a note of warning. Many people will see these differences as insurmountable barriers. Some will use them as an excuse to do nothing or continue business as usual. But I will show how each difference, while containing challenges, is actually a huge opportunity for innovation.

Difference 1: Mental maps

When Hans Monderman says, 'If you want motorists to behave like they are in a village, then build the village', he has a richer resource to work with than what we have in our cities. He simply needs to fan the embers of a centuries old pro-urban tradition that is still deeply ingrained in

The task of liberating our suppressed need for a sense of 'home' may be easier than we think.

the culture.

By contrast, those of us living in Australia or North America must overcome a deeply ingrained anti-urban bias. Now this may sound like a hopeless task. But it is actually a wonderful opportunity. Regardless of where we were born or raised, every human being has a deep hunger for attachment and a sense of home. The revolution we are seeing in many of our cities, with large numbers of people embracing a pro-urban, metro lifestyle is not being fed because all these people have gone to Europe and liked what they have seen. It is feeding into an integral part of the human psyche – our need for a sense of home and roots. In fact, our over-valuing of mobility has caused this need to be suppressed for so long that it is crying out for attention and expression. The task of liberating this suppressed need may be easier than we think. In one sense our task may be simpler than it is for Hans because there is more subconscious pressure for change.

The first step in reclaiming streets as dual-purpose spaces is to reclaim it in our heads and in our culture – a change in the mental topography. Residents in Australia and North America will not use their streets as outdoor living rooms while they believe in their heart of hearts that the only function of streets is to move cars. This means that in our cultural setting (as opposed to the setting that Hans Monderman is working in) we must give much greater weight to working in the mental and social domains than in the physical domain. Don't get me wrong, design is important. But in our situation, I believe that design must be subservient to working in the mental and social domain. In saying this, I do not believe that what we are involved in here is 'social engineering' or 'social

This Dutch home has all the magic ingredients for creating mental speed bumps: a seat out front, no curtains, a window display and historic buildings reflected in the glass.

I am not asking people to embrace some new view of the world but to embrace fully their existing needs.

manipulation'. We are not trying to coerce people into renouncing their current belief system and adopting some radical new belief system. The way I see social change programs is as follows. As I have already said, we all contain contradictory needs and values. Our need to travel and our need to reside are both legitimate needs and deeply rooted in our psyche. When we ignore or suppress a legitimate need, life becomes 'unbalanced' and a 'problem' emerges. Traffic problems are not caused by the fact that we have a desire to move and travel. They are caused when, as a total society, we are not balancing this need to move and travel with the contradictory need for home and nurture. The social programs I design are not built on the notion of tearing down the dominant voice or dominant values. Cars and traffic are not my enemies. My job is to articulate and legitimize the suppressed voice, the value and need that the person already has but which is not getting a fair hearing. I am not asking people to embrace some new view of the world but to embrace fully their existing needs. The programs I design are always built on celebration, the celebration of a suppressed need.

Difference 2: Streets are corridors rather than rooms

Because our streets have been constructed as corridors rather than rooms, the redesigning of our streets is a different kind of a challenge to what it is in the European setting. Once Europeans scrape away the confusing messages, they find an outdoor living room buried under all those traffic control devices. If we do the same, we will almost always find a corridor. This means that changing our streets into rooms is a greater creative challenge.

Again this is an opportunity that opens up some wonderful design possibilities. The greatest redeeming feature of our streets may turn out to be their over-designed width. This often wasted space gives us the opportunity of creating mixed-use neighbourhoods and outdoor living rooms without needing to tear the existing urban fabric. The wasted space in residential streets could easily be recycled into other uses – convenience store, telecommuting centre, library, news stand, flower stall, coffee shop, artist's lofts, hairdresser, or home-delivery depot. Leasing or selling select portions of this space could pay for the entire rebuild of streets into genuine outdoor living rooms, meaning that the retrofitting of these neighbourhood streets would not cost the city a cent. Placement of the buildings could be used to break the corridor up into rooms and create entryways into these rooms. One-way lanes of traffic either side of an activity zone in the centre of the street makes crossing the street much easier and slows traffic significantly. Las Ramblas, in Barcelona, even has restaurants on the sidewalk side of the street with seating in the centre of the street. Waiters with trays of drinks and meals move back and forth between the traffic, acting as great mental speed bumps.

The greatest redeeming feature of our streets may turn out to be their over-designed width.

Las Ramblas, in Barcelona where some restaurants have their seating in the middle of the street.

There is also a lot of wasted space on arterials. In the USA, road diets (taking a four lane road and reducing it to three lanes – one lane in each direction and creating a centre turn lane) is all the rage. Engineers have discovered that this arrangement can actually increase the carrying capacity of a road while reducing accident rates. It is the intersections that control capacity and road diets simplify intersection control. Road diets create a redundant lane that can be put to some other use. However, the only thing that engineers can think to use this reclaimed space for is corridor/movement-related infrastructure – bike lanes, parking, widened sidewalks, or centre median. There is virtually no discussion on how this space may be used for room/residing infrastructure that would foster a more vibrant community life, which would act as a mental speed bump in the corridor.

There is virtually no discussion on how this space may be used for room/residing infrastructure that would foster a more vibrant community life.

Some design professionals may be concerned about the costs of retro-fitting all the streets in a city into outdoor living rooms After all there is not enough money for traffic calming, let alone a wholesale retro-fitting of streets.

I have three responses. Building the social life of streets is the most important step in making them feel more like a room and less like a corridor. Having someone reading a book in a rocking chair in their parking bay will make the street feel much more like a living room than some $500,000 city sponsored beautification program which still leaves the street destitute of people. Recall a time where you have been in a very homely room. What made it feel homely? It probably had very little to do with the actual design of the floor, walls and ceiling. It probably had more to do with the earthy, open spirit of the residents. The personality of the

The amount of money spent has nothing to do with whether a room is warm and inviting and feels like a room.

occupants was probably impregnated into every detail of the room. The occupants may have been very poor and so the furnishings and art were modest and improvised. There were probably tell-tale signs of everyday life scattered around the room: a half-finished child's drawing on the floor, the crayons laying where they were left; a basket of washing half folded; and a coffee mug on the coffee table. Now think of a room that did not feel homely. Chances are the occupants employed an interior decorator to design the room. A lot of money was spent on this room. But there were no telltale signs of every-day life. The amount of money spent has nothing to do with whether a room is warm and inviting and feels like a room. If there is limited budget, then simply putting in some activity nodes (seating, things for kids to climb on, outdoor chess sets) could make an enormous difference to making a street feel more like a room.

My second response to the cost objection is that the wasted space in our streets has a huge economic value that can be captured to pay for very radical rebuilding of the street. I explore this further in Sarah's story. As an aside, on the cost objections, when I show pictures to engineers in Australia or North America of a Hans Monderman street rebuild, they respond: 'Oh we could never afford brick roads like that'. But amazingly, the Dutch need to rebuild their streets every 5-10 years due to subsidence (which may account for why they have been 20 years ahead of everyone else in street design). I asked the Mayor of Haren how on earth they could afford to build these quality streets, not just once, but every 5–10 years. He replied, 'It is a matter of priority. We believe that quality streets are what make us more economically competitive than the next town'.

My third response is that we are ignoring three of the most valuable resources any city has: the altruism of its citizens, resourcefulness of the citizens, and creativity of the citizens. Altruism is giving something to the collective life of the city and expecting nothing in return. Why are we so afraid to ask residents to contribute to the vitality of the public realm? Why can't we ask residents to use their private land for public good? Why can't we ask artists to make great public art and donate it to the city? Resourcefulness is the ability to take waste and turn it into something of value. Cities are fond of handing everything to residents on a silver platter. But often if you give communities a very small amount of money they will make it stretch a hundred times further than the city authorities could ever have stretched it. Creativity is the ability to conjure something out of nothing. If residents were taken on as partners in the retro-fitting of their streets, who knows what methods they may find to finance the project.

If residents were taken on as partners in the retro-fitting of their streets, who knows what methods they may find to finance the project.

Difference 3: Segregated uses

Generally speaking, our cities have highly segregated land uses with neighbourhood streets having only one type of use: housing. By contrast, traditional European streets contain a dynamic mix of uses: shops, homes, work places, schools, and churches. These mixed uses not only reduce journey lengths, they help generate a dynamic street life with people moving by foot or cycle to these nearby destinations. Our mono-use suburban streets make it much harder to generate a dynamic street life.

Again this difference suggests some opportunities and strategies for both cities and residents.

The first thing to note is that, in the traditional city, many of the resident's exchange needs were met spontaneously in the street. This greatly reduced their need to travel for these exchanges. For example, when children play spontaneously in the street, their need to be driven to organized sporting events is reduced. When elderly people can sit and socialize in the street, their need to be picked up in a senior citizens bus and driven to a senior citizens hall for some social activity is reduced. When adults can socialize informally with their neighbours in the street, their need to drive to formalized socializing events is reduced. Building the infrastructure to at least begin to facilitate this spontaneous exchange is very cheap and can actually be done by residents themselves. It requires simple things like seats, shade, drinking water, art, community notice boards, outdoor chess sets, and community bread ovens. Or some simple

Activity nodes invite people to linger and become an 'anchoring presence' in the street. Activity nodes can be easily created by residents themselves.

structures for kids to climb on.

I call this kind of infrastructure 'activity nodes'. Nothing attracts people to a public space like the presence of other people. When we are looking for a coffee shop or restaurant we will tend to go to the one that has already got people in it rather than the one that is empty. So the people who go and do their work in a coffee shop, or read a book in the coffee shop are doing the coffee shop a great service. They become an 'anchoring presence' that attracts other people into the coffee shop. In a similar way, streets need an anchoring presence that will attract other people into the street. The only way to get people to linger and act as an anchoring presence is to create activity nodes. For example, simply putting in some seats may encourage some elderly people to sit in the

Nothing attracts people to a public space like the presence of other people.

street. This may then make it feel safe for some parents to let their kids play in the street. The seats can kick-start a virtuous cycle.

The second thing to note is that there is no denying that having mixed use in the neighbourhood will greatly increase the potential for this spontaneous exchange and further reduce people's need to travel. As already indicated, the incredible width of our residential streets offers the opportunity to reclaim some of this space for other uses.

Difference 4: Arterials our true centres of urbanity

The fourth difference is that in our cities, our arterials are our true centres of urbanity. This is where we find a mix of uses – shops, homes, schools, offices and churches. Yet our cities have had a policy of calming traffic in

Christiansfield, Denmark

the mono-use residential areas and forcing this traffic onto the arterials, thus creating traffic sewers that degrade the real centres of neighbourhood life.

This provides a golden opportunity for cities to use the shared space design principles, currently being pioneered in Europe. In Christiansfield, Denmark, a major intersection was seeing an average of three fatal or serious injury accidents per year. The new design (see opposite):

The paving design in the churchyard is extended across the street so you literally feel like you are driving through the churchyard.

— Removed all traffic control devices.

— Squared the corners (rounded corners and slip lanes encourage traffic to move faster and is unfriendly to pedestrians).

— Made the space feel more like a 'town square'.

— Created a 'room' by using changes in paving to create a border around the room. This sense of enclosure was reinforced by the squaring of the corners and the placement of the pedestrian-oriented lighting poles right on the four corners of the room. In other similar projects in Europe, the entryways to a 'room' are often marked with a change in pavement that gives subtle visual and auditory clues. Sometimes these entryways are raised just slightly, not as much as a traditional speed table, just enough to give the driver the slightest indicator that they are entering a new space. The airspace above the entryway can also be exploited to give a sense of passing through the city gates.

In the three years since the Christiansfield installation, there has not been a death or serious injury. The most surprising outcome for the Danish Traffic Directorate is that the number of traffic backups during peak periods has decreased.

One technique used on major arterials in Europe is to integrate the street into adjoining landuses so the street becomes an extension of the school, church, or park. You feel like you are driving through the church yard or school yard, not on a major road. In Holland there are examples where school play equipment is deliberately placed right on what was formerly the boundary between school and street. The Dutch also use paving to blur the boundaries between pedestrian, cycle and motor traffic space. They reduce curb heights to a minimum. Use chamfered curb edges rather than square. Do away with curb edges all together and have street and sidewalk at the same level. They often extend the sidewalk pavement colour and texture into the street to create the allusion of a much narrower roadway and a much wider sidewalk.

Some other clues as to what can be done on arterials and residential streets are:

— Place activity nodes at intersections. This creates the maximum chance for spontaneous exchanges because it is where pedestrian flows intersect. The concentrating of human activity at these points also creates mental speed bumps at the point where motorist need to be slowed most.

— Blur the boundaries between private and public space. Encourage private landowners to use their private land to contribute to the vibrancy of public space. Encourage them to spill these activities out into the street.

Please remember that these are not fundamentalist design rules but some general guidelines. Where you deviate from these guidelines, you need to make the entire design work as a unit. Each neighbourhood node on an arterial should have its own personality.

I suspect that in the long term we will abandon the policy of channelling traffic onto these arterials and will create a system that defuses traffic throughout the entire street system, with an emphasis on keeping this traffic moving at a very steady pace rather than stop-starting.

Cities will also develop policies of reducing traffic levels in the entire system by helping residents manage their car use more efficiently. Twenty years ago cities accepted that all the trash in the waste stream needed to be there and that you simply built bigger and better landfill sites. But cities suddenly realized that 50%–80% of the waste did not even need to be in the waste stream. Exactly the same inefficiencies are present in the traffic stream. It is utterly feasible for cities to reduce traffic levels by 50% over a ten-year period using resource management techniques.

The boundary between sidewalk and roadway has been blurred by removing the curb and using the same brick colour in both areas.

Difference 5: Where does the city begin and end?

Hans argues that the transition zone from traffic world to social world should be as small and sharp as possible. This is reasonably easy in a Dutch village, but even there the boundary is not always clear. However, in our cities, the edges are even more blurred with malls, big-box stores and huge parking lots littering the edges of our cities for miles, often placed at off-ramps from a freeway.

In my lectures and workshops I emphasize over and over again to both city authorities and residents a basic resource management technique – you always pick the low hanging fruit first. The success you gain from picking this fruit gives you the platform to pick the fruit a little higher. The fruit at the top of the tree is picked last. Humans are strange creatures in that we constantly look at the fruit at the top of the tree and say, 'We can never reach that'. So we do nothing. Alternatively we invest large amounts of energy trying to reach this fruit at the top of the tree and leave the low hanging fruit to rot. I believe that this fifth difference is definitely a piece of fruit at the top of the tree that will take care of itself when we have addressed the first four differences, which are the lower hanging fruit.

But if you force me to speculate about how we may end up handling this issue, my guess is that the first step will be a new kind of 'design signature' for these roads – tree-lined boulevards or even art corridors. I then see the day when many of these malls will fail economically (partly due to the emergence of the neighbourhood economy) and they will be converted into urban villages. The entryway to the larger city will be marked by passing through a series of small villages that were formerly malls. I suspect some cities may even call this the Malls to Villages Strategy.

Practical Action for Residents

The core concepts we have discussed in this book that impact how residents can tackle traffic problems themselves are:

— The speed of traffic on residential streets is governed to a large extent by the degree of psychological retreat of the residents.

— Intrigue, uncertainty and humour create mental speed bumps, subconsciously slowing motorists down.

— Traffic is first and foremost a social and cultural problem, not a design problem. If we had an outbreak of civility, most of our traffic problems would evaporate.

— People who linger in the street provide higher levels of intrigue and uncertainty than those just passing through. They also attract other people out into the street. For people to linger there must be 'activity nodes', such as seating, play areas, art, shade, sunshine, stores.

— The design of a street sends a subconscious message to motorists about the primary purpose of the street and the degree of intrigue and uncertainty likely to be encountered. Streets that look, feel and act as a corridor say to motorists that the space is part of the traffic world. But streets that look, feel and act as an 'outdoor living room' say that the street is part of the social world in which motorists are welcome, but as a guest.

These initiatives range from the extremely easy – requiring virtually no time investment – to those that require a larger time investment.

These core concepts give residents a range of initiatives they can implement as an individual, with their neighbours, or in partnership with their city. These initiatives range from the extremely easy – requiring virtually no time investment – to those that require a larger time investment. These initiatives fall into four basic categories and form what I call the RRIR strategy:

— Reclaim your street as socializing space.

— Relax, move gently.

— Intrigue travellers.

— Retro-fit your street as a room.

Your city may or may not permit some of the activities listed below. Check at www.traffictamers.com to see if your city has registered how they support residents in taming school and neighbourhood traffic. If they are not listed you will need to contact your city directly. While your are visiting the Traffic Tamers web site, you can check out what other cities are doing to empower their residents to tame traffic. You can also see examples of what other residents and neighbourhoods are doing.

Some hints

Move some of your normal activities closer to the street: Instead of reading a book in the sun at the back of the house, read the book in your front yard, or on the sidewalk or in the car-parking space. Instead of painting your furniture in the garage, paint it in the parking bay. Have a dinner party on the sidewalk or in the parking bay. Take note of how these simple activities not only slow traffic but act as a catalyst for the revitalization of your neighbourhood life.

What Residents Can Do To Tame Traffic

- Very easy
- Moderately easy
- Harder
* Details in *Some Hints*

Reclaim your street as socializing space
- Move some of your normal activities closer to the street. *
- Supervise children playing on the sidewalk or in the street.
- Stop and say hello to people in the street.
- Welcome motorists as a guest. *
- Hold a street reclaiming party. *
- Organize social events (street games competition, promenade, etc.)

Relax, move gently
- Walk, cycle, roll, stroll, amble, linger, engage.
- Teach your kids to walk or cycle.
- Reduce your car use to a minimum. *
- When you drive, drive gently. *

Intrigue travellers
- Wave to motorists.
- Do something to make yourself or your vehicle eccentric.
- Put something intriguing in your front yard.
- Put something intriguing in the street. *
- Blur the boundary between your private home and the street. *

Retro-fit your street as a room
- Create activity nodes on your private land* or in the street.
- Connect activity nodes into adventure trail or promenade. *
- Encourage existing local businesses to connect with the street. *
- Encourage new local businesses in your neighbourhood.
- Make your street more like a room. *
- Work with your city to reduce traffic control devices.
- Work with your city to make your street feel more like a room.

Welcome motorists as a guest: If you have a problem with speeding traffic in your street, discuss with your neighbours how you can build a more civil relationship with the drivers. Wave. Give them cake and cookies, invite them to a party, play them music or entertain them. They won't act like a guest unless you treat them like a friend.

Street reclaiming party: Preferably don't close the street to traffic, since this is a demonstration of how neighbourhood life and traffic can coexist quite happily in the same space. Talk about the ways that you as residents have retreated from your street. Experiment with putting that retreat into reverse. Don't put up signs telling motorists what is happening. Condense your activity into the smallest area possible.

Simply reading your book on the sidewalk rather than in your backyard helps to tame traffic in your street.

Reduce your car use to a minimum: Put a pad on the fridge and save up your non-urgent trips and combine them into a single trip. Look for the closest destination (check the yellow pages). Use home deliveries. Walk or cycle to some destinations as a way of getting your exercise. Join a car-share club if there is one in your city.

If you drive, drive gently: Deliberately drive within the speed limit. Be courteous to other road users. See yourself as the vanguard of an outbreak of civility. Put a Pace Car sticker on your car so those behind know why you are driving courteously. Do something funny to your car to make people smile.

Put something intriguing in the street: If you don't own a car, put something unusual in your car-parking space, such as landscaping on wheels, chickens, seating, a chess set, a lounge, sculptures or kids' art.

Blur the boundary between your private home and the public realm: If you have a front fence, take it down. Put something in your front window that contributes to the public realm. Take down your curtains. Put something in your front yard that contributes to the public realm. Make part of your front yard an activity node.

Create activity nodes on your private land: Put something in your front yard that encourages people to stop and linger: a meeting point, seats, a drinking fountain, a dog water bowl, sculptures, play equipment for children, a community notice board or a community bread oven.

Blurring the boundary can be as simple as personalizing your entryway.

Connect activity nodes into adventure trail or promenade: Adventure trails enable children to reach important destinations like the school, library or corner store safely while still having adventures along the way. Encourage private individuals and businesses to adopt the activity nodes along the way. Encourage people – especially senior citizens – to sit out in public space, especially during the hours that children walk to and from school. This builds an informal social network that makes it safer for the children to walk without them needing constant adult supervision. Alternatively, the activity nodes can be connected into a promenade loop and adults can be encouraged to promenade at certain times.

Residents can easily create an Adventure Trail by putting things that will engage children in their front yard or on the sidewalk.

The fish forest ruins

I am currently renovating my front yard as a demonstration of how to use private land for public good. It is on a major route to a local school, so will also become the first activity node of an adventure trail. Left is how it was. Above is the concept drawing I showed my neighbours. It includes water features for children to play in, a drinking fountain, sculptures and community bread oven.

Encourage existing local businesses to connect with the street: Show local businesses that if they create activity nodes outside their store, they are likely to attract more customers. This can be as simple as some seating, but may be some rocks for kids to climb on or an outdoor chess set. Encourage your fellow neighbours to support local business as they help reduce traffic volume and help make your street more lively.

You could encourage a Mr. Coffee to set up in your neighbour-hood. It is a great way to generate social activity in your street.

The same design principles that make a great room make a great street.

Use art, furniture, landscaping and design elements to make your street more like a room: The same design principals that make a great room make a great street. Create entryways. This may be as simple as landscaping in a trailer placed opposite each other at the start of the street and a colourful banner overhead. Give your room a sense of enclosure with landscaping, parked cars, or art. Give your room a 'ceiling' with landscaping, banners, flags, or lights. Use the floor design to help define the room. Put furniture and art in your room. Leave some telltale signs of everyday life – children's toys, a hopscotch square, a basketball hop, a rocking chair with a book on it, a dining table set ready for dinner.

Practical Action for Cities

Cities do not need to abandon their existing Traffic Calming or Safe Routes to School programs to use the techniques I have outlined in this book. I have arranged these initiatives roughly in the order of ease with which cities could implement them. However I believe the order also reflects the order of priority for most modern cities. Many of these initiatives can be put in place under existing regulations and within existing departments. The initiatives are grouped under three categories: Social Programs, Street Design, Spatial Planning.

Many of these initiatives can be put in place under existing regulations and within existing departments.

Social Programs
Stop solving traffic problems for the community. Instead, empower residents and children to take responsibility for solving traffic problems themselves.
— Create a *Do It Yourself Traffic Taming Kit* that is given to all residents who complain about traffic in their street. Tell them that if this self-help approach fails to resolve the problem to their satisfaction, then the city will investigate design interventions further. Everyone in the city, including police, should have a standard response to traffic problems. (Visit www.traffictamers.com to see how your city can adapt existing Traffic

Tamers materials to create such a kit. It even has an email service that the city can adapt as its standard response to traffic complaints.)

— Integrate a social program such as the Neighbourhood Pace Car or the Traffic Treaty into the Traffic Taming Kit. Make stickers or treaty forms available.

— Encourage residents to participate in psychologically reclaiming their streets. Give incentives for residents who remove front fences, create activity nodes, or participate in social programs such as the Neighbourhood Pace Car.

— Inform residents about what things they can and can't do to tame

There are many ways residents can help make their street feel more like a room and less like a corridor. These flags create a 'ceiling' and make the space more intimate. The city needs to relax regulations and inform residents about what they can legally do.

Portland, Oregon, has passed special regulations that allow residents to rebuild intersections as a 'neighbourhood plaza'. This includes painting murals on the street surface and erecting structures such as community notice boards and seating. This structure is a memorial to a cyclist killed at this intersection.

traffic. Tell them if they need a permit. Find ways to reduce regulation and red tape. You can publish these guidelines on the Traffic Tamers web site so residents have clear guidance. This information on the Traffic Tamers web site is easily linked to your city web site.

— Remove regulations that prevent street games or social activities in the street.

— Officially change the name and function of parking spaces outside people's homes from 'parking spaces' to 'multi-use spaces'. Allow these spaces to be used for a wide range of activities.

The same design principles that make a great indoor room make a great outdoor room. In this Santa Monica street, the banners create a 'ceiling' and the landscaping create the 'walls'.

Street Design

— Rationalize and minimize existing signage and traffic control devices. (This can be done without a commitment to removing all traffic control devices).

— Give residents a 'blank canvas' for them to reclaim their street. A blank canvas gives the residents a designated area in which they can create activity nodes or street reclaiming devices, and gives them permission and perhaps the materials to 'paint' the canvas. A blank canvas may be two bare poles at the entry of the street that residents are encouraged to convert into an ever-changing entryway. Or it may be markers on the road that show residents the space they can convert into whatever they like. Or the blank canvas may be placing Universal Anchoring Devices in the street so the residents can create their own art that plugs into the anchoring device (see opposite for details). The Universal Anchoring Device gives the city control over where devices are placed but gives the residents the ability to create their own art or even swap art with other neighbourhoods.

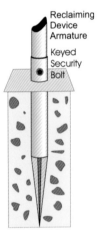

Reclaiming Device Armature

Keyed Security Bolt

The Universal Anchoring Device allows residents to create their own street art. It also means residents can have an ever-changing streetscape. Art is easily moved around the city.

— Where possible, replace signage with 'non-literal' forms of communications. Instead of a sign warning that there is a school ahead, make it feel like the driver is going through a school grounds. Use sculptures and art to indicate the presence of cyclists or children playing. Include elements that contain high levels of intrigue.

— Where a more traditional traffic calming approach is still being taken, do not use elements that overtly punish the driver. Instead, change the geometry of the street by installing positive, community building infrastructure – a seating area, play area or a business kiosk. Focus on making the street look more like an outdoor living room and less like a traffic corridor.

— As the social life in the street increases, reduce standardized traffic control devices to clearly signal the amount of uncertainty likely to be encountered.

— Actively redesign streets to be more like rooms and less like corridors. Blur the boundaries between the various functions of the street. If such a street is designed for a 20–30 kph speed, you may find that you can circumvent many of the onerous demands of your design regulations – compulsory signage, frangible elements on the sides of the road, etc. It is

The floor pattern can be used to break a street, designed as a corridor, into a series of discrete rooms.

legitimate to argue that the lack of traffic control devices is an important element in creating a 20–30 kph environment.

— On major arterials or highways through towns, use road diets to reclaim space and use the saved space to make alternative modes of transport more attractive, and create activity nodes that will build the social life of the street.

Spatial planning

— Find ways to encourage a greater mix of uses in residential streets. This does not necessarily mean rezoning existing residential uses. It may mean recycling excessive street space into exchange space.

— Encourage land use changes on major strip development areas on the outskirts of town. Actively encourage the conversion of malls into villages. Create villages with distinct entry and exit points. Prevent further strip development.

In my opinion, if cities invest in working with the mental and social realm, then the design of the physical realm will begin to take care of itself. Humans are incredibly creative, especially when they want to give expression to their deepest dreams As noted earlier, for too long cities have ignored three important resources of its citizens – altruism, resourcefulness and creativity.

Liability

The major objection I get to using mental speed bumps to tame traffic is liability. Yet exactly the same issue was raised when I first promoted traditional traffic calming. After all, traffic engineering had been based on removing anything that hindered the quick passage of vehicles, not putting obstacles in their way. Even today, many cities shy away from traffic calming for fear of being sued. Yet the facts do not back the perception.

In an article *Legal Status of Traffic Calming*, Reid Ewing reviews data from nearly 50 cities with traffic calming programs in the USA and found only two successful lawsuits against traffic calming programs, and one of these was overturned on appeal. (*Transportation Quarterly, Vol. 57, No.2, Spring 2003, pp11-23*). Reid Ewing explains why there have been so few successful cases:

> *In both case and statutory law, the distinction is made between discretionary functions (which are generally immune from tort claims) and ministerial functions (which are not). Discretionary functions involve a choice among valid alternatives. Ministerial functions involve operational decisions that leave minimal leeway for personal judgment.*
>
> *The decision to spend public funds on traffic calming, or to install one set of measures versus another, or to design measures for one speed versus another, is discretionary. The duty to warn motorists of traffic calming measures that require slowing down, or to maintain measures in a safe condition, or to construct measures per design specifications, is ministerial…*
>
> *Under sovereign immunity, courts will not second-guess discretionary decisions of public officials if there is any reasonable basis for them.*

The choice to use mental speed bumps over other forms of traffic control is discretionary and therefore not open to litigation. This does not mean that the city can remove signs warning of speed bumps and not the speed bump itself. This kind of uncertainty is 'bad uncertainty' and opens the city up to litigation.

The other major area of litigation is suing for damages on traffic calming devices that have not been properly maintained or not properly signed. However, the intrigue and uncertainty approach does not use devices such as speed bumps that can potentially damage a vehicle. There is therefore no need for signs and the potential for damage through not

The choice to use mental speed bumps over other forms of traffic control is discretionary and therefore not open to litigation.

*Mental Speed Bumps
is not a new concept.
Ancient city build-
ers had it down
to an artform. By
observing, we can
discover their secrets.*

properly maintaining infrastructure is greatly reduced. Not only will the city save money on traffic control devices, but it should also save money on litigation.

The only potential area of litigation that may result from the approach outlined above is if someone runs off the road and collides with a street-reclaiming device such as a sculpture or banner pole. In the early stages, the use of the Universal Anchoring Device (UAD) should overcome this potential problem. The UAD allows the city to nominate where street reclaiming devices are placed and maximum dimensions for those devices. It may even be possible for the UAD to be designed so that it sheers off if struck with sufficient force.

In the USA there is no design manual with set standards for traffic calming. Many practitioners fear that having no design guidelines will open them up to liability. Reid Ewing asks, 'In the absence of standards, what is to immunize traffic calming programs against legal challenges'? His answer is 'a rational planning and implementation process' because being able to demonstrate a rational approach is important in tort liability and substantive due process cases.

It is therefore important for cities to adopt a rational and orderly planning process for the introduction of ambiguity, intrigue and uncertainty as a means of reducing traffic speeds and building the community and economic life of the city. In the section on False Sense of Security, I argued that maximum safety is achieved when the environment sends a clear message about the amount of unpredictability that is likely to be encountered. A rational planning process must therefore involve a partnership with the community – a building of a vibrant street life at the same time as traffic control devices are reduced and other design elements are introduced that mark the street as an outdoor living room rather than a corridor. This means there must be a strong social program element to this strategy, not only to get residents to relate to their street in a different way, but to relate to their car in a different way.

A rational and orderly planning process will probably start with residential streets, school streets and neighbourhood activity nodes such as local shopping centres, particularly those on arterial roads. This is where the False Sense of Security is likely to be very high (high levels of unpredictability in the environment but high levels of predictability signalled by the design). These areas will benefit most in safety terms from the introduction of ambiguity into the street design. A rational and orderly planning process may require a gradual reduction in traffic control devices, not a blanket overnight removal.

A rational planning approach may also require setting up some trial and experimental areas to demonstrate how this approach actually works. It will be important, not just to measure traffic speeds and accident rates in these areas, but to also quantify any improvements in the vitality of community life.

PART 3

Sarah's Story

Building a Bridge to the Future

It started with a simple brochure in my letterbox announcing a public meeting to discuss plans to 'upgrade' a major road through my neighbourhood in Brisbane, Australia. I left the meeting a committee member of Citizens Against Route Twenty. A week later, I found myself media spokesperson. I had no previous experience in community activism, no tertiary education, no interest in traffic and urban planning, and no idea about politics.

Full of incredible optimism, I started my new job with a six-hour door-knock along the proposed route. At every door I knocked on I got the same response: 'Once they (the state government) have decided to do something, there is nothing you can do to change it'. I was stunned by this sense of resignation and powerlessness. Even our committee didn't believe we could win. 'We will give them a good fight', I was told, 'but we can't win'. I was probably the only one in our entire community naive enough to believe we could win.

The reason for this pessimism was that the Bjelke Peterson Government had been in power for over 20 years and ruled via a gerrymander. They could do what they liked in the big cities because they only required the country vote to stay in power.

But in creating the stories, we had built a bridge in our imagination from 'here' to 'there' and suddenly the impossible had become possible.

I was outraged, but didn't have the foggiest idea of what to do. Out of sheer desperation I suggested to the committee that we spend a half-day pretending we had won. I suggested we make up stories about how we won and that these stories should start from our current reality.

On the day we pretended we had won, we invented a whole lot of stories about how it happened. We then chose the story that seemed most plausible and decided to build our campaign strategy on this story.

Something significant happened during our half day of play. The committee changed its tune from 'we can't win' to 'maybe we can'. Prior to us playing 'let's-pretend-we-have-won', there was no obvious road that could take us from current reality to our desired future. But in creating the stories, we had built a bridge in our imagination from 'here' to 'there' and suddenly the impossible had become possible. And we had a rough mud map to guide us.

Three years later we won the impossible battle, and it happened largely according to the story that we had created three years earlier when we played 'let's pretend'.

A few years ago I met someone in Atlanta who was doing a thesis on 'the politics of the possible'. I thought it was a fascinating subject. How is the ceiling of what is possible in a community set? Why can Dutch cities rebuild their streets in brick every five to ten years, but we can't do it once? Why is one community locked into envisioning a future that is the same as today, while another community believes they can create a future that is very different to today? One of the things that puts a glass ceiling on the possible is the degree to which we allow rational, linear thinking to dominate the playful dreamer and storyteller. Many people will read this book and say, 'that is impossible where I live'. But it is only impossible because you have no stories of how it may happen.

I imagine a future in which speeding in other people's neighbourhoods will be just as antisocial as blowing smoke in someone's face. I imagine children once again playing in the street and elderly people sitting in the street sharing their life wisdom with others. I imagine vibrant cities full of intrigue and humour. Here is my story of how it happened in my part of the world. Please feel free to expand and change the story. Write yourself into the plot. Make yourself the main character if you please. If you don't like my story, write your own. Send it to me. I may even put it in the next edition of this book.

Make yourself the main character. If you don't like my story, write your own.

Two Misfit Mutts from Australia

Historians call it the Great Civility Outbreak – a cultural revolution in which it became the social norm to be 'civilized' and 'a good citizen'. It was a revolution in attitudes that was even greater than the revolution in attitudes to smoking that preceded it. Among other things, it spelt the end of speeding traffic in neighbourhoods, speed bumps, front fences, and trivial liability suits. The trigger for this social revolution, according to some historians, was the first Corridors to Rooms International Conference. Others credit the book you now hold in your hands. But I know the story behind the story.

Sarah Yabanka was five when she moved to Timboona with her mother, father and elder brother, George. Her dad had been promoted to regional manager for a large parcel delivery service. Six months after arriving in Timboona, Sarah's mum got a job as a radiographer at the hospital. The Yabanka household was an extremely busy household. Every morning at 6:10 Mrs Yabanka would wake the children. Breakfast was and 6:45. Mr Yabanka took the red sports utility to work at 7:15. At 7:28 Mrs Yabanka would herd Sarah and George into the silver four-wheel-drive, and psychologically prepare to do battle with the 350 other parents trying to drive their kids to school. 'The city should do something to sort out this traffic mess', she would often mumble to herself. 'Some kid is going to get killed here one day. If there wasn't so much traffic I would allow the kids to walk the six blocks to school. No wonder we have an obesity problem'!

It was one week after Sarah's ninth birthday that she got an email from her cousin Samatha who lived in another state. Samatha had discovered a really wicked website that she thought Sarah should check out. She told Sarah that she had just become a licensed Traffic Tamer and wanted to know if Sarah would join her in a bit of cousin rivalry to see who could earn the most Magic Stars. So Sarah clicked the link in her email and ended up on the Traffic Tamers web site where she met Red, Fleet and the Traffic Taming Wizard.

Red and Fleet turned out to be two misfit mutts from Australia who had started a club to make streets safer for kids. They had enlisted the help of the Traffic Taming Wizard to teach kids the three magic ways of taming traffic. Kids could earn Magic Stars each time they used these magic spells to help make streets safer for kids. Sarah thought the coolest part about Traffic Tamers was that kids got to train adults and give them a certificate if they passed the test. 'Cool, I get to give mum and dad a test', Sarah said to herself.

Sarah emailed Samatha to say she accepted the challenge.

The first thing she needed to do to start earning Magic Stars was walk to school, well at least the last ten minutes of the journey. But her mother flatly refused. 'Sarah, the streets are simply too dangerous'.

'But that is the point Mum, I need to walk to help make the streets safer so other kids can walk'.

How to Tame Dragon Wagons

1 Rest your Dragon Wagon

Wild beasts do not hurt you if you leave them to chill out in their favourite haunt. If you leave your Dragon Wagon at home in the garage it will not kill or injure anyone!

Dragon Wagons get very cranky if they are overused.

DRAGON DEN

DO NOT DISTURB!

Let your dragon wagon rest in bed. Have a walking adventure instead!!

2 Calm your Dragon Wagon

Wild beasts pick up our vibes. If you are calm, they are calm. If you rush, they rush. And when Dragon Wagons rush they are very dangerous.

Leave early. Be calm. Get adults to turn their car into a Pace Car!

Dragon Wagon, Dragon Wagon, Play my game, Take 3 deep breaths (ahh, ahh, ahh) Now your calm...

I'm calm... and setting the pace!

PACE CAR

3 Intrigue Dragon Wagons

Wild beasts are curious. They become less agro if they are not bored and have something interesting to look at.

Keeping motorists intrigued gets them to drive slower, without them even knowing it! It works like magic.

wave wave

Do I know him?

Her mother pondered this for a moment.

'Come and look at the web site', Sarah pleaded. 'It has a special section explaining to parents why it is so important for kids to walk to school. Besides, I want to beat Samatha'.

'Get your father to look at it. He's better with technical things'.

That night over dinner, Mrs Yabanka asked Mr Yabanka if he had looked at the web site for Sarah.

'Yeah, it makes a lot of sense', he replied. Sarah's dad ground lots of pepper onto his mashed potatoes. Sarah could never understand why he liked so much pepper. 'Sarah and George are probably missing out on some really important stuff by being driven everywhere. I remember walking to school. We would…'.

'But times have changed Malcolm', Sarah's Mum cut in.

'True'. Sarah's dad put even more pepper on his potatoes. 'But not all change is good'.

'Well I think it is irresponsible for us as parents to risk our children's lives like that', Mrs Yabanka stated. Sarah's heart sunk. When her mum got that look in her eye, she knew that she was highly unlikely to change her mind.

Sarah's dad put down his fork. 'Tell you what Dear. I will start work half an hour later for the next two weeks and walk with Sarah and George. That will ensure you earn two Magic Stars, hey Sazza'.

Sarah squealed with delight and jumped up to give her dad a huge hug. 'Oh daddy! You are the best daddy in the world'.

'My pleasure, Sazza. Who knows, maybe we will have some adventures together'.

For the next two nights, the main topic of conversation at the dinner table was the adventures Sarah, George and Mr Yabanka had while walking to school. The first day they saw a bird's nest in a tree with a magpie feeding three squawking babies. Sarah and George were fascinated and it had never occurred to Mr Yabanka that his kids were missing these kind of real-life nature lessons. The second day they found someone's shopping list. They had a great time making up stories about whose shopping list it may have been. They worked out that the owner of the shopping list had a dog with a flea problem and that either the dog or the owner liked chocolate-coated almonds.

'Did you have any adventures when you walked to school?', George asked his mum.

'Sure, almost every day'. Mrs Yabanka stopped eating and looked into space for a brief moment. 'It was not really on the way to school but when we were coming home. I remember there was an old tumbledown house about five blocks from where we lived. We would take a detour and approach the house on tiptoes, heart racing, expecting a wicked witch or ghost to grab us as we scampered past. One day Betty, my best friend, dared me to go and knock on the door. I only got halfway up the path when the big front door creaked open. I don't think our feet touched the ground all the way home'.

Using the Devil to Tame the Devil

Sarah sat at the dinner table fiddling with a piece of paper. 'What have you got there, Sazza?', asked her dad.

'Well, this afternoon I went to the Traffic Tamers web site to find some more ways for me to earn Magic Stars. And I printed this out for you and mum to sign'.

Mr Yabanka read the paper very thoughtfully. 'So you want to train us how to tame our Dragon Wagons Sazza?'

'Yep! And I want you to turn our two cars into Pace Cars. You sign a pledge to drive within the speed limit for one year and we put a sign in the back window to let the other drivers know why you are driving courteously'.

Mrs Yabanka came into the room at this point and Sarah's dad handed her the information sheet about the Pace Car.

'I'm not sure about this Sarah. I mean, it is a great idea, but I cannot imagine myself driving everywhere within the speed limit – especially not in the four-wheel-drive with its super-smooth ride. Why you don't even feel speed bumps in that thing', she exclaimed.

'So don't you want to help us kids make streets safer Mum?'

That night Sarah's mum helped her make the signs for the back of the two cars.

The next night, over dinner, Sarah's mum reported that she had caught herself speeding three times. 'But I noticed so many more things about the neighbourhoods I drove through, things I had never noticed before. I think I will have to start leaving a couple minutes earlier to take the pressure off myself'.

Six days after the Yabankas had started walking to school, there was a knock at their front door. It was Mr Thompson. 'Your daughter introduced my daughter to this program called Traffic Tamers. She has convinced me to let Cynthia walk. But I am a single dad, and I was wondering if Cynthia could walk with you and your children'.

Mr Yabanka agreed. 'Mind you, I don't think it will be too long before they have enough experience to walk themselves. What would

make it much safer is if less parents were driving their kids – and if we all drove a little slower'.

Mr Thompson agreed to turn his car into a Pace Car.

After dinner, Sarah approached her father: 'I think it is time our entire school class took the Traffic Tamers Challenge. Would you talk to our teacher about it and volunteer some time to make it happen?'.

And so it was that not just Sarah's class, but the entire school became involved in the Traffic Tamers program. After completing the Traffic Tamers Challenge, Sarah's class decided they would undertake the Big Adventure where the class gets to design its own challenge. Sarah's class decided they would aim to sign up 400 Pace Cars and make them part of their Class Fleet.

'That is a lot of Pace Cars', Sarah's dad said when she reported back what the class had decided.

'Well dad, I told them I could get at least 148'.

'One hundred and forty-eight? How the hell do you expect to sign up that many by yourself?' Sarah's dad quipped.

'Because', Sarah looked her dad lovingly in the eye, 'that is how many cars you have at work'!

'And how are you going to get the rest of them'?

'Well our class has made a special Do-It-Yourself Traffic Tamers Kit for adults and we are going to get our parents to hold a Traffic Tamers Street Party and sign up everyone in the street'.

'Mmmm, I see, very ingenious Sazza'.

'Yes. I said our street would do it first. I really love you heaps Daddy'.

The Street Party

Three of the Yabanka's neighbours came over on a Wednesday night for some drinks. It was the first time any of them had met, other than to nod hello. The conversation was a little stiff until Sarah presented the group with the Do-It-Yourself Traffic Tamers Kit. Inside the box was a bucket of chalk, a ball, some personal messages from children in her class and a DVD. The DVD explained to the group why the speed of traffic on their street was governed to a large extent by the degree of their psychological retreat from the street, and how they could psychologically reclaim their street. It showed them, step by step, how to organize a Traffic Tamer Street Party.

As the DVD finished playing, Sarah suddenly jumped to her feet. 'I've got an idea. To get everyone excited about the Street Party, let's show everyone in the street the DVD. We could project it onto the side of our house and get everyone to bring their chairs and sit on the sidewalk to watch it'.

'Great idea Sazza. You are a genius'. Sarah's dad gave her a big wink.

And it was a stroke of genius because after watching the DVD, the neighbours came to the street party knowing exactly why they were there.

They began by talking about the ways they had retreated from their street. Even while they were discussing this, people commented that the traffic seemed to be going much slower. Someone suggested that because the speed of traffic was slower, they should move the conversation from the sidewalk to the parking bays on the side of the street. As soon as they did this, the speed of traffic dropped even further. They discussed how they could make their street look more like a room and less like a corridor.

'If we had some banners, we could create a ceiling for our room', someone commented.

'Well in Italy they hang their washing over the street. That sure makes you feel like you are in someone else's outdoor living room', said another.

'Lets do it right now!', a few exclaimed.

While the washing was being strung over the street, a number of people took up their positions as 'Welcoming Hosts'. They offered motorists coffee and cake on a plate and explained why they were having a street party. They even invited the motorists to join them and a couple took up the offer. The kids used the chalk to create temporary murals on the street. Each time a car came along, someone would call 'car' and everyone would stand aside to let it through.

Sarah and a couple of her friends from her class went around getting people to sign the Pace Car Pledge. 'With the 148 we got from dad's work, and the 26 from Malinda's mother's work, and the 32 we got today, we now have 208, over halfway to our goal already', Sarah explained excitedly to her mum.

People began discussing ways to continue reclaiming their street.

'You know this is not about traffic speed', Mrs McWattle, a delightful 86-years young commented. 'This is about the quality of our neighbourhood life. When I was a kid, we used to play in this street and there was a seat on the sidewalk where my mother would sit to shell peas. And while she shelled her peas she would chat to a couple of old people who lived in our street. It seems like they were always on that seat. They were the guardians of our street'.

'We should put a seat in our street', piped up Sarah, who had been absorbed in Mrs McWattle's story. 'We could put it outside our house and make it a very special chair, couldn't we Daddy'?

Blurring the Boundaries

'I'm not sure Sazza', Mr Yabanka ground some pepper onto his dinner. 'I'm not sure the city council will just let us put a seat on the sidewalk'.

Sarah thought for a moment, 'Well we could put it in our front yard'.

'Don't be silly', retorted brother George, 'we've got a big high brick fence. No one would see the seat behind the fence'.

'No, I mean we would knock the fence down first. I mean fences are boring. There is nothing intriguing about a fence and we need lots of intrigue if we are going to get motorists to go slower and make streets safer for kids. And I think we should invite everyone in the street to help us knock it down! It would be a good excuse for another street party'.

Four weeks later, the residents of Carnation Street joined together in knocking down the Yabanka's front fence. They recycled the bricks to create a paved area. Ms Zelta, a metal sculptor, had created a brightly coloured seat with an extremely high back that reminded Sarah of fireworks exploding in a night sky. Mr Cando owned a nursery, so he wheeled two big palms in azure blue pots up in his wheelbarrow. Mr Brandville, a plumber, created a simple drinking fountain and dog-drinking bowl.

The sun was beginning to set when Sarah went down and knocked on Mrs McWattle's door.

'Your special seat is ready. I have even brought you some peas to shell'.

As Mr Brandville opened a bottle of champagne, he commented, 'You know, this really blurs the boundary between your private space and the public street. It certainly makes the street much more interesting'.

'Well, here's to a lot more blurring of the boundaries', said Mrs McWattle raising her glass. With that she squeezed Sarah's hand and they rubbed cheeks. Sarah and Mrs McWattle sat there shelling peas until it got dark.

This was the first of many Blur the Boundary Parties in Carnation Street.

The Promenade

There was a loud knocking on the Yabanka's front door. 'Is the seat out the front of your house for sale?', asked the total stranger.

'Ah, no', Sarah's mum was obviously taken by surprise at the question. 'Actually I'm not really sure who owns it. Ms Zelta down the street made it, it is on our land, but it kind of belongs to the whole street'.

'Ah well, no harm asking', responded the stranger, 'but it is a fantastic piece of art'.

At this point Sarah had another of her bright ideas. 'Mum, what if Ms Zelta sold the seat to the man and she made a new one for our yard. That way we could have a different seat'.

That afternoon the fireworks seat was gone from the Yabanka's front yard. Ms Zelta had some money in her pocket. And she had a very bright idea.

There were twelve houses on Carnation Street that had now had their boundaries blurred. Nine of them agreed to allow Ms Zelta to display her sculpture pieces in their yards. They would get wonderful art for free, she would make a living, and the street would have an ever-changing streetscape.

Ms Zelta decided to have an opening of her new 'gallery'. In order to create a buzz she decided to concentrate the opening hours – from 5 pm to 7 pm three nights a week for two weeks. To give her gallery a little more atmosphere for the opening, she created some banners to hang over the street.

While Ms Zelta was erecting the banners, a reporter from the local current affairs television program happened to drive down the street. She stopped to ask Ms Zelta what was happening in the street. The next night, Carnation Street, with its blurred boundaries and outdoor gallery was the lead story.

Mrs McWattle sat with Mrs Yabanka on the seat outside the Yabanka's, watching the passing parade of people and cars. 'Ironic isn't it', commented Mrs Yabanka, 'we started out wanting to calm the traffic in

our street, but because we did such a good job everyone is driving here to look at our street!'.

Mrs McWattle thought for a moment. 'You know, it really isn't a problem. The traffic is going so slowly even I feel safe crossing the street. Much better than when there were not so many cars but they were going a million miles an hour. Besides, this is so much better than sitting inside, watching re-runs of Neighbours on the telly'.

When the two-week gallery opening was finished, the residents of Carnation Street were discussing the experience.

'The life in our street over the past two weeks reminds me very much of what it is like in Spain in streets created especially for promenading', Mr Bloomsberry said.

'I think we should encourage residents and visitors to keep walking up and down our street in the evening hours', added Mrs McWattle.

'OK, but lets just do it one night a week so we keep it fresh and vibrant', someone added.

Everyone agreed to make it every Wednesday evening. But even when it wasn't Wednesday there were lots of people promenading in Coronation Street.

Jumping Beans

Wendy was a single mother who lived at number 86 Carnation Street. She worked part-time as a pastry cook, but really needed to increase her income, since raising three daughters was proving expensive. One Wednesday she was sitting on one of the benches with Mrs McWattle watching all the people walking past. Mrs McWattle was telling Wendy stories about street life when she was a kid. 'You know dear, the butcher use to bring his meat van to the street and carve the meat in the street. And the mothers would stand around the cart and exchange news. Then someone would say, "Would you all like to come back to my place for a cup of tea"? Yeah, home-deliveries were a big part of the street life back then. We had the fruiterer – I remember riding on the back of his cart while he whistled a tune. Then there was George the Grocer, you would put your order in the week before and he would literally get you anything you needed – candles, kerosene, brooms – he would even order in pots and pans'.

Suddenly Wendy had her big idea. Jumping Beans. A mobile espresso bar that she could wheel out during the promenade hour.

Wendy was only renting her premises so she asked the next door neighbours, the Johnsons, if they minded her using their blurred bound-

ary. She decided to put up special lighting so that even in the winter months, when days are shorter, people could still enjoy good coffee and cakes.

Jumping Beans was an instant hit. Wendy soon expanded her opening hours from just Wednesdays to include Sunday mornings when she also put out newspapers. In fact, Wendy was doing so well she decided that she could probably give up the job at the cake shop. Why make cakes for someone else to sell when she could now sell them herself.

One balmy Tuesday, Wendy was strolling down Carnation Street when she saw Mr Bloomsberry sitting on one of the seats in the blurred boundaries, deep in thought.

'Mind if I join you?' she asked.

'No, be my guest. How's Jumping Beans going?'

'OK, but I have run out of seating room. Even the parking spaces outside the Johnson's are chock-a-block full'.

'Have you thought of using the centre of the street?', Mr Bloomsberry suggested.

'We couldn't do that – could we?' Wendy responded in a defeated tone.

'Well in Barcelona, I saw places where the restaurants are on the sidewalk and the seating is in the middle of the street. The waiters carry their lattés and cakes across the traffic lane to the seats. Honest, I've seen it with my own eyes and I even took pictures. I think it is ingenious because it makes a very skinny lane of traffic on either side of the sitting area, which is really easy to cross. It makes the traffic go pretty slow'.

'But is Carnation Street wide enough?' queried an excited Wendy.

The Dominos Fall

Wendy and Mr Bloomsberry explained their plans to the city engineer. They showed him the pictures from Barcelona. They referred the engineer and city planner to the Traffic Tamer web site to explain why introducing some intrigue and uncertainty into the street would actually make the street safer. They explained that they were not asking the city for any money. Mr Cando, the nursery owner, had offered to provide all the landscaping free of charge. Wendy agreed to put a small advertisement on the menu cards and to sell the pots and plants for Mr Cando, a kind of win for them both. The city finally agreed when Mr Bloomsberry said they were prepared to make it a six-month trial with a comprehensive review at the end of this time. After all, if it worked and was used in other streets, the city could save millions of dollars in traffic calming costs.

Mr Bloomsberry sat working on his laptop computer at one of the tables now located in the centre of Carnation Street.

'What are you working on?', Wendy put the latté down and stood with her hand on her hips.

'Work stuff. Because of modern technology, I can work from home two days a week now. It's great. But I do miss the human interaction of the office, which is why I am sitting out here working'.

'Ironic isn't it', Wendy replied, 'kind of staring into the past and the future simultaneously. Mrs McWattle talks about the good old days when mums stayed home and the delivery man provided a point of social interaction for the mothers. A bit like the village well in older cultures, I guess. Then the mothers all got jobs so there was no delivery man and no life in the street. Now we have the technology for both men and women to work from home. Maybe everything will go full circle and we will get the delivery man back again'.

Creating a room in the centre of the street was a piece of cake. The potted plants carved out an intimate space.

'Fascinating insight Wendy', mused Mr Bloomsberry. 'I know on the days I work from home, I could do with a little more social interaction, which is why I spend so much time here. I reckon this neighbourhood could do with a neighbourhood office. You know, good Jumping Bean cakes and coffee, but with a photocopier, fax machine, scanner, and Internet points for our laptops. That would mean I could avoid going to the office another one or two days a week. Jumping Beans could become the new village well!'. Mr Bloomsberry became very excited as the light bulbs flashed on in his head. 'Jumping Beans could even accept home deliveries for the people who are at work. When they come home they could just pop into Jumping Beans and pick up their deliveries'.

'Interesting thought', Wendy replied. 'Now that the City has given its blessing to us keeping the seats in the middle of the street, what is stopping us from having a building in the middle of the street? Didn't some of those streets in Barcelona have buildings in the middle of the road'?

'You are absolutely right Wendy. Imagine if we had a building at each end of the street. It would create a wonderful sense of entry into our street plus provide a protected public promenading space right in the middle of the street'.

'And what if the City sold or leased the land for the building'? Wendy suggested. 'That could pay for creating a wonderful public socializing space in the centre of the street. It would be a cost-free transformation of our street from a corridor into an outdoor living room'!

From Little Things…

Sarah's thirtieth birthday party was at Jumping Beans on Carnation Street. Wendy and Mr Bloomsberry had opened six Jumping Beans in other parts of Timboona.

'It seems so long ago', said Sarah's mother with a slight lisp, caused by a mild stroke six months earlier. 'It is hard to remember the days when people would just jump in their cars and drive somewhere without even thinking. There are very few cars on Carnation Street now, and they all go very slow and respectfully'.

'I was reading a story about it the other day Mum, and they called it the Great Civility Outbreak'. Sarah sat looking into space for a moment. 'Remember when I first joined Traffic Tamers and I wanted to walk to school. You flatly refused to let me'.

'Well in those days, we thought things were the way they were because that's the way they were. We never thought about how we might be able to change things just by making a very small change in our lives', Mrs Yabanka reflected.

'Hey Sarah, remember the day you asked mum and dad to sign the Pace Car Pledge'? George, her brother chipped in. 'Remember Mum's reaction, "I just can't imagine driving everywhere within the speed limit…

not in that four-wheel-drive".' Everyone laughed as George imperson-
ated his mother, 'The speed limit feels like a crawl in that thing. Why,
you don't even feel the speed bumps'!

Wendy delivered a tray of drinks. 'Hey Sarah, remember the day
everyone got together and took down your front fence and created the
first blurred boundary? Remember the fireworks seat? And I will never
forget the look on old Mrs McWattle's face when you sat her in that seat
and presented her with a bowl of peas to shell. Priceless'!

'Old Mrs McWattle, bless her soul', Sarah's eyes moistened. 'I just
can't imagine that before we began blurring the boundaries in our street,
that she spent all her time indoors, watching re-runs of Days of Our
Lives and Neighbours. Once those seats went in, she seemed to
be there all day, everyday. She would stop me as I walked past
her to school and whisper in my ear, 'Thanks dear, you have
made a big difference'.

Wendy returned to serving as the group continued remi-
niscing. 'Guess what'? Sarah interjected, 'I met the guy who
started Traffic Tamers. He gave a talk on innovation and creativity at this conference I attended last week. He talked about
how yesterday's innovations are today's problems and that
today's innovations will be tomorrow's problems. He
eventually replaced Traffic Tamers with another innovation. But what was really strange was that he said
that his inspiration for the Traffic Tamers program was
a nine-year-old girl called Sarah who lived in his imagination. Don't you think that's a weird coincidence that my

name is Sarah and that I joined Traffic Tamers aged nine?'.

At that moment Wendy returned with a cake and 30 candles.

Mr Yabanka rose to his feet with his glass, 'I want to propose a toast'. He paused and looked his daughter in the eye, 'Sazza, history may never record how the Great Outbreak of Civility started. But we all know, because we were there. Here's to the little seeds from which big things grow. Here's to the imagination of my little girl'.

Acknowledgements

There is no way I could have developed the core concepts in this book without the contributions of thousands of people. My mind is part of the 'collective commons' and the products that grow there belong to the entire community.

It would be impossible to thank everyone who has contributed to my growing understanding –the list would be too long. But I do need to thank a number of people for their help with Mental Speed Bumps.

Hans Monderman – for spending time showing me projects and opening his mind to me like a great evolving book.

Ben Hamilton Baille – for support and putting me in contact with Hans.

Ingrid Burkett – for being a best mate and intellectual travelling companion.

Mind Matters Participants, Copenhagen, 2004 – for spending a whole day challenging my thinking and stretching me. Hope you recognize some of your wisdom within these pages.

The following people read a first draft of Mental Speed Bumps and made a range of invaluable suggestions: Emily Richmond, Phil Smith, Andrew Stuck, Ewa Bialecka, Bronwen Machin, Heidi Schallberg, Anne Franklin,

Don Schneider, Cathy Turner, and Angelika Schlansky.

Thanks to Diane McIntosh for the cover concept and helping to refine the design.

Finally, thanks to Rod Ritchie for editing the book.